The Ultimate Insiders

Newswork   3

The Ultimate Insiders
U.S. Senators in the National Media

Stephen Hess

The Brookings Institution
Washington, D.C.

Copyright © 1986 by
THE BROOKINGS INSTITUTION
1775 Massachusetts Avenue, N.W., Washington, D.C. 20036

Library of Congress Cataloging-in-Publication Data

Hess, Stephen.
  The ultimate insiders.
  (Newswork; 3)
  Includes bibliographies and index.
  1. United States. Congress. Senate—Reporters and reporting.
2. Press and politics—United States.
I. Title. II. Series: Hess, Stephen. Newswork; 3.
JK1274.H47   1986   328.73′071   85-48177
ISBN 0-8157-3598-7
ISBN 0-8157-3597-9 (pbk.)

9 8 7 6 5 4 3 2 1

THE BROOKINGS INSTITUTION is an independent organization devoted to nonpartisan research, education, and publication in economics, government, foreign policy, and the social sciences generally. Its principal purposes are to aid in the development of sound public policies and to promote public understanding of issues of national importance.

The Institution was founded on December 8, 1927, to merge the activities of the Institute for Government Research, founded in 1916, the Institute of Economics, founded in 1922, and the Robert Brookings Graduate School of Economics and Government, founded in 1924.

The Board of Trustees is responsible for the general administration of the Institution, while the immediate direction of the policies, program, and staff is vested in the President, assisted by an advisory committee of the officers and staff. The by-laws of the Institution state: "It is the function of the Trustees to make possible the conduct of scientific research, and publication, under the most favorable conditions, and to safeguard the independence of the research staff in the pursuit of their studies and in the publication of the results of such studies. It is not a part of their function to determine, control, or influence the conduct of particular investigations or the conclusions reached."

The President bears final responsibility for the decision to publish a manuscript as a Brookings book. In reaching his judgment on the competence, accuracy, and objectivity of each study, the President is advised by the director of the appropriate research program and weighs the views of a panel of expert outside readers who report to him in confidence on the quality of the work. Publication of a work signifies that it is deemed a competent treatment worthy of public consideration but does not imply endorsement of conclusions or recommendations.

The Institution maintains its position of neutrality on issues of public policy in order to safeguard the intellectual freedom of the staff. Hence interpretations or conclusions in Brookings publications should be understood to be solely those of the authors and should not be attributed to the Institution, to its trustees, officers, or other staff members, or to the organizations that support its research.

Foreword

IN 1977, when Stephen Hess began the studies that were to become the Brookings series called Newswork, most books on newsgathering in Washington took the form of journalists' memoirs, interesting largely for their anecdotal richness rather than for analysis of the part played by the news media in the governmental process. But the events of the 1970s, notably those that now bear the collective name of Watergate, made it obvious that the press could no longer be thought of as merely a conveyer of information. Things changed because reporters were there. The moment, therefore, was particularly appropriate for Hess, a senior fellow in the Brookings Governmental Studies program and an experienced observer of the gathering and dissemination of news in Washington, to examine how the press fit into the public life of the capital.

In the first volume of Newswork, *The Washington Reporters* (1981), Hess surveyed over half the Washington-based journalists and asked questions about their backgrounds and work habits, their freedom to choose their own stories, and the means they used to get information. In the second volume, *The Government/Press Connection* (1984), he investigated the jobs of public information officers at five executive agencies and considered their efficiency, relations with reporters, and influence on the news that was reported. Together these two books show the interactions that create news as well as the way events look from both sides of the briefer's podium.

In *The Ultimate Insiders* Hess focuses on the relationships between the national media and the Senate, particularly on which senators are covered and why some are deemed newsworthy and some not. He examines whether certain positions or personality characteristics invite extensive coverage and whether biases exist within the news media. A companion volume, which he is now writing, will continue Brookings special contribution to investigations of the news system in Washington by looking at the relationship between the Senate and local news media.

Brookings received grants for this research from the Cissy Patterson Trust Fund, the Gannett Foundation, the American Broadcasting Company, the Earhart Foundation, and the National Press Foundation, and is grateful to the trustees and officers of those institutions for their generosity. Hess especially wishes to note that the Earhart Foundation of Ann Arbor, Michigan, has supported the three volumes of this series, and wishes to thank Richard A. Ware, who retired as its president in 1984, for a decade of encouragement. The National Press Foundation, which has supported two studies, also has special importance to the author because the grants are given by working journalists.

Helpful critiques of this manuscript were provided by David S. Broder, Timothy E. Cook, Gary C. Jacobson, Samuel H. Kernell, Wayne Koonce, Thomas E. Mann, Paul E. Peterson, and Steven S. Smith. Additional materials were provided by David H. Weaver, director, Bureau of Media Research, Indiana University; Robert E. Peterson, Jr., superintendent, and the staff of the Senate press gallery; Max M. Barber, superintendent, and the staff of the Senate radio and television gallery; Lance Morgan, press secretary, and the staff of Senator Daniel P. Moynihan; the Republican Conference of the Senate; and Laura Walker, Susan A. McGrath, and their colleagues in the Brookings library.

The Brookings interns who assisted the author were Stephen E. Davis (Harvard), Michael F. Flanagan (Cornell), Janet A. Hatfield (St. Lawrence), Hugh J. Hurwitz (Rochester), Nancy Kates (Harvard), Jung M. Lee (Georgetown), Robert C. Lehrman (St. Lawrence), Eric Lipton (Vermont), Ilene G. Lovesky (Middlebury), John H. Sharon

III (Connecticut College), Susanna Sigg (Georgetown), and Gene B. Sperling (Minnesota). The author wishes to thank the Washington Semester at American University and Georgetown University's Institute of Political Journalism for supporting his work through their internship programs.

Pamela D. Harris, Deborah Johanson, and Nancy K. Kintner provided the logistical support for this study. Diane Hodges and Ruby R. Paredes were the administrative supervisors.

The author is grateful to James R. Schneider, his editor, for creative suggestions on organizing the material and other editorial services.

All the views in this book are those of the author and should not be ascribed to the persons or institutions acknowledged or to the trustees, officers, or other staff members of the Brookings Institution.

Bruce K. MacLaury
President

April 1986
Washington, D.C.

For Liz and Pat

Author's Note

LATE AFTERNOON in mid-September 1984. Senator Gary Hart walks down the Capitol steps on the Senate side, crosses the parking lot, and leans against a low stone wall, tilting his face into the last rays of a still-warm sun. He is alone, waiting for William Cohen, his colleague from Maine with whom he is writing a novel.

"Senator, the last time I saw you here you were surrounded by fifty reporters." (It had been February. He was then a presidential candidate and the networks were waiting for him to comment on the death of Yuri Andropov.)

Hart laughs. "Fame is fleeting."

"Is this symbolic?"

"It would make a good opening scene for your book."

Senator Hart is right. For what this book seeks to illuminate is why reporters surround certain senators, while others can walk down the Capitol steps unnoticed. Is it just that fame is fleeting? Are reporters merely fickle? The Constitution may say that all senators are equal, but the press says that some are more equal than others. This is a study of the national media's coverage of U.S. senators—when and why. Yet I had not always meant it to be that.

The second session of the Ninety-eighth Congress convened at noon on January 23, 1984, lasted for 264 days, and adjourned sine die on October 12. During that period the Senate met for 131 days, and for almost all of those days I was there, walking the halls of the Capitol and the three Senate office buildings, riding the Capitol subway, looking for senators who would let me ask them questions as we walked along, going to their committee hearings and press conferences, listening to their floor debates and to their interviews with reporters, talking to press secretaries, and hanging around the press galleries with the reporters and asking them questions. From my notes I would construct a book about the Senate and the press. It is the book I will write next. It will describe the culture of the Capitol Hill press corps, including such oddities as how the reporters govern themselves in the congressional press galleries. It also will focus on those reporters that are the most important to the senators who wish to get reelected, the local reporters who explain the senators to their state's voters.

On the days when the Senate was not meeting in 1984, especially during the summer when most of political Washington was away at the presidential conventions, my interns and I used our time compiling records—in some cases from data that the Senate had filed away and never bothered to tell researchers about—of the number of TV cameras in committee rooms, for which committees, when; of which senators send their press releases to the radio and television correspondents' galleries, how often, about what; and which senators appear on the public affairs programs and which are interviewed in the television gallery's studio. We found other information in more conventional places. We counted and coded the adjectives used to describe senators in newspaper stories, the number of times senators appeared on network news, what they talked about, and how often they were mentioned in major newspapers. Other researchers have had similar curiosities, and we wanted to compare our findings with theirs.

Our conclusions were substantially removed from the prevailing view among social scientists and special enough, I feel, to stand as a separate book. The national media, notably the television networks, have been increasingly described in terms of a Circe luring a group of lusty legislators away from their obligations to create consensus and coherent policy. In analysis after analysis, the national media have been listed among the causes for destabilization and instability in the Congress. It is an emphasis, as we shall see, that is wrongly placed.

This study focuses on high-prestige national news outlets—a handful of newspapers and newspaper groups, wire services, newsmagazines, and television and radio networks. Excluding those on the staff of *Congressional Quarterly*, the specialized magazine that is an important source for other news outlets in reporting congressional activities, the number of full-time national reporters on Capitol Hill is under a hundred,[1] although at times of heavy activity news organizations will add to the regulars. Most, but not all, cover both the Senate and the House of Representatives. Though the number of national reporters may be modest, their impact is thought to be considerable. Presumably they are the ones of whom a political scientist wrote, "the mass media are powerful agenda-setters. Media choices about which stories to emphasize and how to treat them have a substantial impact on the determination of which issues will be seriously considered and which will not."[2]

Students of Congress are becoming increasingly interested in the news media, a useful and long overdue addition to their

1. Of those news outlets whose coverage is computed in this study, in 1984 the Associated Press had a Capitol Hill bureau of fifteen reporters under the direction of Tom Raum (and there were ten AP "localizers" who cover state delegations); United Press International and Steve Gerstel had eight reporters (and a separate regional staff of six). The *Wall Street Journal*'s congressional reporters were Dennis Farney, David Rogers, and Jeffrey H. Birnbaum. The *New York Times* had two full-time reporters, Martin Tolchin and Steven V. Roberts, with Jonathan Fuerbringer almost full time, to cover the budget (and another reporter, Jane Perlez, whose assignment was the New York delegation). The *Washington Post* had Helen Dewar reporting from the Senate and Margaret Shapiro from the House. The *Los Angeles Times* reporters were Paul Houston and Karen Tumulty, the latter also covering the California delegation. The *Christian Science Monitor* was represented by Julia Malone. The three television networks each had three correspondents, although one was usually away covering presidential or other elections, with the leading congressional stories most often reported by Phil Jones (CBS), John Dancy (NBC), and Ann Compton (ABC). Other news organizations that regularly provide national coverage from Congress include Reuters, *Washington Times*, Baltimore Sunpapers, *Chicago Tribune*, *Boston Globe*, *New York Daily News*, *Journal of Commerce*, Cable News Network, AP Radio, UPI Radio, NBC Radio, Mutual Broadcasting, National Public Radio, *Time*, *Newsweek*, *U.S. News & World Report*, *National Journal*, Gannett, Scripps Howard, Newhouse, and Cox.

2. John W. Kingdon, *Congressmen's Voting Decisions* (Harper & Row, 1973), p. 210.

investigations. This book, however, is essentially about the press, not about the Congress, although the cast of characters includes U.S. senators. When I add up senators' interviews, press conferences, and the number of times they are mentioned in the media, it is because reporters have written about them. This is the third volume of a series called Newswork, and, as such, its focus is on senators as the subjects of journalists. Why do reporters find some senators of more interest than others? Why do reporters find some senators of no interest at all? The political scientists who study Congress would ask other sorts of questions: How do the news media treat the Senate as an institution? How do senators seek to use the media to advance their personal goals? Such findings will be welcome. There is much to be learned about relations between Congress and the press when approached from either direction.

The lesson of this study for Gary Hart and his colleagues is not really that fame is fleeting nor even necessarily that reporters are fickle (although both propositions are correct). Rather, it is that the national news media need senators as representatives; they are to be covered as categories, not individuals. Thus in February 1984 Gary Hart stood for Potential President, a category of considerable interest to the national press corps; in September 1984 he was not in one of the categories that determine newsworthiness, which explains why when he walked down the Capitol steps he was confronted by a lone researcher.

S.H.

Contents

Tables

I

The Media Accused

THE EDITORS of U.S. News & World Report chose this title for an article in their April 23, 1984, issue: "EVEN CONGRESS IS UNHAPPY WITH CONGRESS." It was a view reflected in other headlines that year:

SENATORS ASSAIL ANARCHY IN NEW CHAMBER OF EQUALS
New York Times, November 25, 1984

SENATE FACES INSTITUTIONAL IDENTITY CRISIS
Washington Post, November 26, 1984

By the end of 1984, U.S. senators and the journalists who cover them were in agreement. "Often the Senate is inexplicable. Just as frequently it is incapacitated. More and more, senators worry that it is becoming increasingly irrelevant," wrote Helen Dewar, Senate correspondent for the Washington Post. "A decade of diffusion of authority has steadily eroded the powers of seniority and leadership, creating near anarchy," according to Martin Tolchin of the New York Times.[1]

A great many reasons are given as contributing to what Alan

1. Dewar, "Senate Faces Institutional Identity Crisis," Washington Post, November 26, 1984; and Tolchin, "Senators Assail Anarchy in New Chamber of Equals," New York Times, November 25, 1984.

Ehrenhalt, *Congressional Quarterly*'s political editor, calls the "individualist Senate,"[2] a body of one hundred members in which each one is following his or her personal, often contradictory, agenda: outmoded rules, too many subcommittees, too much staff, too many roll call votes, too little reliance on political parties to get elected, too much attention paid to lobbyists and political action committees, too few safe Senate seats, too little regard for tradition, and too many unpleasant people getting elected.[3] The individualist Senate may also reflect the times we live in: when the nation lacks consensus, its fragmentation will presumably be reflected in its body of representatives.[4]

In a provocative speech on September 12, 1984, Senator Dan Quayle (R-Indiana) told his colleagues that the basic problems of the Senate were "proliferation" and "trivialization":

> We have proliferated the number of committees and subcommittees, the number of staff, the number of floor amendments, the number of cloture votes, the number of roll call votes, the number of fiscal processes and so forth and so on. At the very same time as we have proliferated, and probably as a consequence, we have trivialized the matters with which we are concerned. We use our processes more and more to emphasize small issues rather than large ones, and that is turning the Senate away from its historic function as the focus of national debate.[5]

Quayle cited a recent defense authorization bill that had 103 amendments. He considered fewer than a tenth of them to be

2. "In the Senate of the '80s, Team Spirit Has Given Way to the Rule of Individuals," *Congressional Quarterly Weekly Report*, vol. 41 (September 4, 1983), p. 2182.

3. A sophisticated view of the present dysfunctionality of Congress is that it is an unanticipated consequence of the congressional reforms of the 1970s. See Burton D. Sheppard, *Rethinking Congressional Reform* (Schenkman, 1985), p. 343.

4. See Bryce Harlow, ("Congress meanders when the American people are indecisive. . . . "), in Albert R. Hunt, "In Defense of a Messy Congress," *Washingtonian* (September 1982), p. 181.

5. *Congressional Record* (September 12, 1984), pp. S10957–S10960, and Quayle's speech of June 28, 1984, *Congressional Record*, pp. S8533–S8536, which includes a compilation by Roger H. Davidson and Walter J. Oleszek of "Selected Proposals for Revising the Senate Committee System." Note, too, the remarks of Senator Thomas Eagleton ("Whereas our rules were devised to guarantee full and free debate, they now guarantee unbridled chaos. . . . "), *Congressional Record* (November 23, 1985), pp. S16476–S16477.

"substantive," and there were certainly too many amendments to receive serious attention. Yet every senator had to have his amendment. Senators had become so "self-important" that no one could take charge, said Quayle, calling for "collective self-restraint,"[6] a view echoed by Professor James MacGregor Burns who thinks that politicians are now engaged in a game that he names King of the Rock.[7]

At some point in all examinations of the decline of Congress, a finger will be pointed at the news media, especially at network television. "What's Wrong With Congress?" asked the cover of *The Atlantic*, in December 1984. In part, Gregg Easterbrook wrote,

> the penalties for being a glory-seeker have been all but eliminated. . . . [W]ith the expansion of television coverage, playing to the crowd has become much more rewarding than playing to the club. . . . While Congress itself is difficult for the networks to cover, individual congressmen make ideal subjects for television. . . . Congressmen, in turn—particularly senators, because of their extra prestige—have found that they can use television to cultivate national followings. . . . Self-promotion has always been a factor in Capitol Hill affairs, but the advent of television has made it convenient to a degree never before possible.[8]

Of the Senate's junior members, Howard Baker (R-Tennessee), then the majority leader, told *New York Times* reporter Steven V. Roberts: "If you don't let them do anything on the floor [of the Senate], they do it on the steps [of the Capitol], and somehow there is always a TV camera out there, and there is always a reporter that will listen."[9] Senator Patrick J. Leahy, the Vermont Democrat, noted that there always have been obstructionists in

6. *Congressional Record* (September 28, 1984), p. S12272; also see the *Wall Street Journal* lead editorial of October 5, 1984, which called Congress a "collection of 535 egos" and urged "some minimal sense of discipline." Senator Quayle was speaking as the chairman of the Temporary Select Committee to Study the Senate Committee System. Unfortunately his committee was then having trouble formulating proposals because schedule conflicts made it difficult to gather enough senators at the same time and place to hold a business meeting, according to Rich Burkhardt, "Senate Committee Bugged By Jinx It's Grappling With," *Roll Call*, September 20, 1984.

7. *The Power to Lead* (Simon and Schuster, 1984), p. 148.

8. "What's Wrong With Congress?" *The Atlantic* (December 1984), p. 64.

9. "Senate's New Breed Shuns Novice Role," *New York Times*, November 26, 1984.

the Senate, but "it wasn't somebody trying to get fourteen seconds on the evening news."

Many serious students of Congress among social scientists have accepted these propositions:

> It became possible [in the 1970s] for any member of Congress to get national coverage and become a nationally recognized figure. . . . This trend toward personal publicity provided, in contrast to the Rayburn era, a range of tangible and possible outside incentives. No longer did a member have to play by inside rules to receive inside rewards or avoid inside setbacks. (Norman J. Ornstein)[10]

> Senators now seek to cultivate national constituencies on their own, receive great amounts of publicity, and are more likely than heretofore to find independent advocacy more satisfying than coordinated legislative activity. (Nelson W. Polsby)[11]

> The networks have discovered that individual congressmen—not only the leaders but also the more colorful and maverick junior members—make for good interviews. So they now appear frequently in the Washington-based interview slots in NBC's "Today," CBS's "Morning News," and ABC's "Good Morning, America" and "Nightline." (Austin Ranney)[12]

> Television has created a new breed of senator and congressman—the carefully coiffed show horse who pushes a few favorite causes but scorns legislative chores and serious homework. (Lewis W. Wolfson)[13]

Michael Robinson, who also argues that "the changes in the media have given younger members and maverick members more political visibility—and consequently greater power—than ever before," further claims that greater reliance on the media in politics "is one sign of a new congressional character—one more dynamic, egocentric, immoderate, and perhaps, intemperate." He quotes a campaign consultant's advice on how to find a successful

10. "The Open Congress Meets the President," in Anthony King, ed., *Both Ends of the Avenue* (American Enterprise Institute, 1983), pp. 201–02.

11. *Congress and the Presidency*, 3rd ed. (Prentice-Hall, 1976), p. 103.

12. *Channels of Power: The Impact of Television on American Politics* (Basic Books, 1983), p. 145.

13. *The Untapped Power of the Press* (Praeger, 1985), p. 40.

candidate: "You get the guys with the blow-dried hair who read the script well."[14]

The consensus among journalists, senators, and scholars, then, is that the national media pay more and more attention to less and less important senators (the mavericks, the junior members, the blow-dried but empty-headed). This focus weakens the Senate's leadership, especially relative to the strength of the leadership in the 1950s, and contributes to decentralizing power within the Senate. Indeed, television even may be changing the character of those who get elected. In short, the consensus declares that the type and amount of national media coverage is producing disturbing changes in the makeup, behavior, and functioning of the Senate.

This study examines the first of these assumptions: it focuses closely, and from various angles, on which senators get covered by the national media, and why. It measures the number of times senators are seen or mentioned on the television networks' evening news programs, the number of times they are listed in the index of national newspapers, the number of times they are guests on major Sunday television interview programs. The study relates these findings to the senators' committee assignments, leadership positions, party affiliations, ideologies, various personal characteristics, and to their efforts to generate publicity through press releases and news conferences. While much of the data is for 1983, the study is given longitudinal depth through reexamination of previous research going back to 1953.

What then does this study discover about which senators are important to the news media beyond the borders of their own states?

—Most senators—between 80 and 90 percent—receive so little attention from the three television networks and other elements of the so-called prestige press that the national news media are irrelevant in affecting their elections or promoting their policies. This is the reality now, and it has been the reality for at least three decades.

14. "Three Faces of Congressional Media," in Thomas E. Mann and Norman J. Ornstein, eds., *The New Congress* (American Enterprise Institute, 1981), pp. 93–95.

—The national news media concentrate their resources on covering the Senate's leaders (a term I use to include committee chairmen and ranking minority members of the committees). The only notable exceptions are presidential aspirants (those expected to seek nomination in the next election year).

—Rather than being a destabilizing and decentralizing force, scattering attention among a wide range of junior legislators, the national news media focus on those senators who seem to wield institutional power. Indeed, the coverage of the national news media from 1953 through 1983 has increasingly directed attention to the definable leaders at the expense of the nonleaders, mavericks, and others. Although political scientists such as Randall B. Ripley have claimed that power among senators since the end of World War II has been moving from an institutional base (position) to a personal base (charm, skill at personal relations, expertise),[15] the national media have not contributed to the movement; they have instead increasingly emphasized institutional power.

—The distinction between show horses and work horses (that is, between those who get publicity and do little legislative work and those who do not get publicity but do most of the legislative work), while once valid, is no longer a distinction the news system makes.[16] Today those who do the work get most of the publicity.

—The "effort factor," evinced by senators who try harder for national attention through better press operations, makes little difference. Most Senate press operations are directed at the local market, where they do make a difference.

—It is not true that television network news promotes a type of senator who is young, attractive, and blow-dried. Few of those who fit this description attract national coverage.[17]

15. See "Power in the Post-World War II Senate," *The Journal of Politics*, vol. 31 (May 1969), pp. 465–92.

16. "The hero of the Hill is not the hero of the airwaves," wrote David R. Mayhew in 1974. "The member who earns prestige among his peers is the lonely gnome who passes up news conferences . . . in order to devote his time to legislative 'homework.' " See *Congress: The Electoral Connection* (Yale University Press), p. 147. Also see James L. Payne, "Show Horses & Work Horses in the United States House of Representatives," *Polity*, vol. 12 (Spring 1980), pp. 428–56.

17. While this study concentrates on the Senate, two other studies, as yet unpublished, reach similar conclusions about the House of Representatives. See

Senate reporters for national outlets, who allowed me to share their working lives for a year, think about their beat in terms of power. They gravitate toward those legislators who are the *Ultimate Insiders*, the ones who call the committee meetings or direct the floor action, or would do so if their party were in the majority.[18] Those senators who refuse to play the power game, who want little more than to serve their constituents' local needs and to get reelected, are of no interest to reporters for the national media.

Senate reporters are interested in potential presidential nominees, but these senators are really in another league: if they do seek the presidency, they will be covered by other reporters. The national political press corps that takes over when a senator goes in search of the nomination writes candidate stories, not senator stories. The focus becomes the horse race, and it makes little difference whether the horses have titles like senator or governor or vice-president. What matters is, are they ahead or behind?[19] So

Timothy E. Cook, "Newsmakers, Lawmakers and Leaders: Who Gets on the Network News from Congress" paper prepared for the 1984 annual meeting of the American Political Science Association (*Legislative Studies Quarterly*, forthcoming); and Joe S. Foote and David J. Weber, "Network Evening News Visibility of Congressmen and Senators," paper submitted to the Radio and Television Division of the 1984 meeting of the Association for Education in Journalism and Mass Communication. I find these works especially significant in the way they relate to this book, not just because of the value of confirmation by careful researchers, but because it has been generally assumed that the effect of the national media has been even more distorting in terms of promoting the maverick House member at the expense of that body's leadership.

18. In her splendid Ph.D. dissertation, Susan Heilmann Miller wrote, "From the press's point of view, the most desirable spokesman . . . is the person who can be taken to represent the largest possible number of people . . . On most matters of public policy, the President is the spokesman for the entire nation—i.e., the ultimate spokesman." This concept reflects mass or quantity as the basis for choosing news sources. When Senate reporters seek the Ultimate Insiders, on the other hand, they are using a qualitative basis for choosing sources, the persons whose names can be attached to information that is most apt to be proved accurate in a chamber of one hundred supposed equals. See Susan Heilmann Miller, "Congress and the News Media: Coverage, Collaboration and Agenda-Setting" (Ph.D. dissertation, Stanford University, 1976).

19. There is a large body of comment on this subject including David S. Broder, "Political Reporters in Presidential Politics," *Washington Monthly* (February 1969); Martin Nolan, "Faust at the Racetrack: Let the Reader Beware," in Frederick Dutton, ed., *Playboy's Election Guide, 1972* (Playboy Press, 1972); Timothy Crouse, *The Boys on the Bus* (Random House, 1973); Lou Cannon, *Reporting: An Inside View*

in presidential election years most column inches in newspapers and seconds of air time that are devoted to senators have nothing to do with the Senate.

Celebrities in the Senate are also no more than a diversion. A senator who rides on the space shuttle or marries a movie star will always make news but will not be the basis for sustained press attention. Celebrities are good for a story on a slow day, not for a generalization—symbolically they do not stand for anything other than themselves, which is why they fade so quickly.

That the average senator is irrelevant to the national media should become abundantly clear as these data unfold. That the national media is irrelevant to the average senator is not a proposition tested here. It may well be that senators and their staffs spend their days plotting to be noticed by Dan Rather, Tom Brokaw, and Peter Jennings, as many seem to believe. This study shows that their chances are almost nil. As experienced politicians, they should have known this already.[20] What this study shows is that the national media make careful rational decisions in judging who is worthy of attention. Yet either our respect for the press or our faith in ourselves as news consumers is so low that this modest conclusion is far from the conventional wisdom.

(California Journal Press, 1977), chap. 9; Stephen Hess, *The Presidential Campaign* (Brookings, 1978), chap. 7; John Foley, Dennis A. Britton, and Eugene B. Everett, Jr., eds., *Nominating a President: the Process and the Press* (Praeger, 1980); and F. Christopher Arterton, *Media Politics: the News Strategies of Presidential Campaigns* (Lexington, 1984), chaps. 3 and 6.

20. For example, a newsletter called *Staff*, published by the U.S. House of Representatives Select Committee on Congressional Operations, May 1978, p. 4, wrote of national television, "Most Members of Congress are never covered throughout their careers. . . . Most national TV news coverage of Members of Congress is initiated by the networks, not the Members, and is limited at best."

II

The Noted Few

ACCORDING TO Senator Robert Byrd (D-West Virginia), "The United States Senate has always attracted some of the great personalities in American history. Towering, eloquent, magnetic, adroit, brilliant, blustering, intimidating, crafty, highminded, haughty, heroic and humorous."[1] But whatever their abilities or the attraction of their characters, most senators are rarely mentioned in the national media. Year after year, session after session of the Senate, reporters from the radio and television networks, the major newspapers, and the newsmagazines focus on only a handful. The Bob Doles and the Mack Mattinglys, the Gary Harts and the Jeff Bingamans, are equal when the roll is called in the Senate chamber, but when attention is paid by the national media, they are undeniably unequal.

The first published effort to examine press attention to U.S. senators was made by G. Cleveland Wilhoit and Kenneth S. Sherrill, who added up the times each senator's name appeared on the Associated Press "A" wire in 1964. Wilhoit and David H. Weaver then compared newsmagazine coverage of senators in 1965–66. The next study by Wilhoit and Weaver, joined by Sharon Dunwoody and Paul Hagner, used various media indexes, including newspapers, popular magazines, and network television for

1. *Congressional Record* (September 7, 1984), p. S10844.

9

1965–66, 1970–71, and 1973–74. The last of these Indiana University-based studies to appear tabulated senators' Associated Press appearances for 1953–54, 1965–66, 1969–70, and 1973–74. Another team, Joe S. Foote and David J. Weber, counted the number of times each senator was mentioned on television network evening news programs during 1981–82.[2] My own calculations used various approaches to 1983 sources.

There is thus a rich history tracing which senators have been of interest, and in what order, to the national media over three decades. In these studies, the ten senators at the top get from 30 percent to 64 percent of the Senate's total coverage; the top twenty senators absorb 49 to 75 percent of the media's attention. Table 2-1 summarizes the results of the studies (for the details, see appendix tables B-1 through B-10). Major fluctuations in the figures in table 2-1 are caused by impending presidential elections in which senators are contenders for their parties' nominations. The most pronounced media concentration on a few senators came in 1964 and in the years immediately before the presidential elections of 1972 and 1984. Indeed, Senator Barry Goldwater (R-Arizona), his party's nominee, accounted for 30 percent of all senatorial coverage in 1964. In years that are not influenced by presidential campaigns the figures are relatively stable.

Although some of these studies focused on network television evening news programs and others on newsmagazines, wire service reportage, or newspapers, it is a tenet of communications research that the national media, whether print or electronic, apply the same values in covering the news and report on the same people and events in roughly the same order. Nor should this be surprising. Almost all the pioneer television journalists—Eric

2. See G. Cleveland Wilhoit and Kenneth S. Sherrill, "Wire Service Visibility of U.S. Senators," *Journalism Quarterly*, vol. 45 (Spring 1968), pp. 42–48; David H. Weaver and G. Cleveland Wilhoit, "News Magazine Visibility of Senators," *Journalism Quarterly*, vol. 51 (Spring 1974), pp. 67–72; David H. Weaver and others, "Senatorial News Coverage: Agenda-Setting for Mass and Elite Media in the United States," in *Senate Communications with the Public* (Commission on the Operation on the Senate, 94 Cong. 2 sess., 1977), pp. 41–62; David H. Weaver and G. Cleveland Wilhoit, "News Media Coverage of U.S. Senators in Four Congresses, 1953–1974," *Journalism Monographs*, no. 67 (April 1980); and Joe S. Foote and David J. Weber, "Network Evening News Visibility of Congressmen and Senators," paper submitted to the Radio and Television Division of the 1984 annual meeting of the Association for Education in Journalism and Mass Communication.

Table 2-1. *Media Coverage of U.S. Senate, Selected Periods, 1953-55 to 1983*

Period	Number of senators	Percent of total coverage	Source[a]
1953-55	Top 10	35	Associated Press
	Top 20	52	
1964	Top 10	64	Associated Press
	Top 20	75	
1965-66	Top 10	45	*Time, Newsweek,*
	Top 20	59	*U.S. News & World Report*
1965-66	Top 10	36	Associated Press
	Top 20	52	
1965-66	Top 10	43	*Reader's Guide to Periodical*
	Top 20	55	*Literature;*
			3 newsmagazines;
			10 large newspapers
1969-70	Top 10	32	Associated Press
	Top 20	49	
1970-71	Top 10	59	*Reader's Guide to Periodical*
	Top 20	75	*Literature*
1973-74	Top 10	34	Associated Press
	Top 20	51	
1973-74	Top 10	30	*Reader's Guide to Periodical*
	Top 20	52	*Literature;*
			4 large newspapers;
			3 TV network news programs
1981-82	Top 10	42	3 TV network news programs
	Top 20	58	
1983	Top 10	50	3 TV network news programs;
	Top 20	68	3 TV Sunday interview
			programs;
			5 large newspapers

a. *Reader's Guide to Periodical Literature* indexes 250 popular magazines. The newspapers used in the 1965-66, 1973-74, and 1983 studies are listed in Appendix B.

Severeid, Howard K. Smith, Walter Cronkite, Charles Collingwood, David Brinkley, John Chancellor—began their careers at newspapers or wire services. And as Chancellor and Walter Mears of the Associated Press note in their primer on the American news business, the stories chosen each day by the wire services, networks, and newspapers "usually are similar and sometimes almost identical" because "seasoned editors looking at the same set of events will come to many of the same conclusions."[3] In an important book comparing CBS and UPI coverage of the 1980 presidential campaign, Michael J. Robinson and Margaret A. Sheehan find interesting qualitative differences between news on television and in print, but whenever their analysis is quantitative—counting seconds or column inches—network and wire service are virtually identical in their coverage.[4] Observe, too, that in appendix table B-12, of the twenty senators who received the most attention from leading newspapers in 1983, seventeen were also in the top twenty on the networks' evening news programs.

In my study, press coverage of senators in 1983 was quantified by considering three aspects of the media: the networks' evening news programs, the networks' Sunday interview programs, and coverage in five newspapers of national reputation.

Using the *Television News Index and Abstract*, prepared by Vanderbilt University's Television News Archives, my researchers and I assigned one point for each time a senator was mentioned and two points for each time a senator appeared on the networks' evening news. (A senator could receive no more than two points for a story.) Using material provided by the networks, we assigned three points for each time a senator appeared on "Meet the Press" (NBC), "Face the Nation" (CBS), or "This Week with David Brinkley" (ABC). The television component amounted to 41 percent of our ranking.

One point was also awarded for each time a senator's name appeared in the *Los Angeles Times, New York Times, Washington Post,*

3. *The News Business* (Harper & Row, 1983), pp. 5–6.
4. *Over the Wire and on TV: CBS and UPI in Campaign '80* (Russell Sage Foundation, 1980). Note, for example, how the CBS and UPI coverage of the Iranian hostages goes up and down in tandem (p. 187).

Christian Science Monitor, or *Wall Street Journal*. This information came from the data base of the *National Newspaper Index*. We then deducted all stories of a local nature (judging from the *Index*'s titles), thereby adjusting the scores of senators from New York, New Jersey, and Connecticut (part of the *New York Times* circulation area), from Maryland and Virginia (*Washington Post*), and, of course, from California. "WILSON NAMES TWO JUDGES TO DISTRICT COURT" was a *Los Angeles Times* story that was not considered in the score of Senator Pete Wilson (R-California), for example.[5]

Each senator's separate score for newspapers, for TV evening news, and for Sunday TV programs can be found in appendix table B-12. However, I believe the composite scores shown in table 2-2 better reflect the homogenized quality of this news, a sort of consensus on a newsmaker's worth as determined by Washington journalists who think of their product in national terms.

Unlike previous studies, which excluded senators who served only part of the period under review, this ranking included Henry Jackson (D-Washington), who died in September 1983, and his successor, Republican Daniel Evans. There are thus 101 names in table 2-2.

In several cases table 2-2 blends notable differences in the attention paid to a senator on television and in print. Majority leader Howard Baker has the highest rating on television but ranks fifth in the newspapers (behind John Glenn, Alan Cranston, Robert Dole, and Gary Hart); Senator Charles Percy, chairman of the Foreign Relations Committee, also does better on television than in newspapers (seventh place among senators in the television ranking; fifteenth place in newspaper coverage). Howard Metzenbaum and Charles Mathias, who are frequently out of step with the Senate's leadership, are rated substantially higher on television than in newspapers. However, just about the same twenty sena-

5. The five newspapers in this study have a combined weekday circulation of nearly 5 million, with the *Wall Street Journal* accounting for almost 2 million and the *Los Angeles Times* and the *New York Times* roughly 1 million each. However, major reportage from all except the *Wall Street Journal* is syndicated and therefore will appear in other newspapers as well. The three television networks' evening news programs on a weekday have a total audience of about 50 million.

Table 2-2. Ranking of Senators by Media Scores, 1983[a]

Top third		Middle third		Bottom third	
Senator	Score	Senator	Score	Senator	Score
Glenn, J. (D-Ohio)	563	Pell, C. (D-R.I.)	31	Hawkins, P. (R-Fla.)	13
Cranston, A. (D-Calif.)	354	Long, R. (D-La.)	31	Inouye, D. (D-Hawaii)	13
Baker, H. (R-Tenn.)	316	McClure, J. (R-Idaho)	31	Rudman, W. (R-N.H.)	13
Dole, R. (R-Kans.)	307	Garn, J. (R-Utah)	31	Melcher, J. (D-Mont.)	12
Hart, G. (D-Colo.)	229	Kassebaum, N. (R-Kans.)	31	Sasser, J. (D-Tenn.)	12
Hollings, E. (D-S.C.)	171	Heinz, J. (R-Pa.)	30	Boschwitz, R. (R-Minn.)	11
Kennedy, E. (D-Mass.)	159	Leahy, P. (D-Vt.)	30	Cochran, T. (R-Miss.)	11
Helms, J. (R-N.C.)	146	Thurmond, S. (R-S.C.)	28	Pressler, L. (R-S.D.)	11
Domenici, P. (R-N.Mex.)	138	Warner, J. (R-Va.)	28	East, J. (R-N.C.)	10
Moynihan, D. (D-N.Y.)	114	Roth, W. (R-Del.)	27	Johnston, J. (D-La.)	10
Jackson, H. (D-Wash.)	112	Eagleton, T. (D-Mo.)	26	DeConcini, D. (D-Ariz.)	9
Tower, J. (R-Tex.)	107	Gorton, S. (R-Wash.)	26	Randolph, J. (D-W.Va.)	9
Mathias, C. (R-Md.)	105	Specter, A. (R-Pa.)	26	Wallop, M. (R-Wyo.)	9
Percy, C. (R-Ill.)	102	Grassley, C. (R-Iowa)	25	Huddleston, W. (D-Ky.)	8
Dodd, C. (D-Conn.)	96	Simpson, A. (R-Wyo.)	25	Stennis, J. (D-Miss.)	8
Laxalt, P. (R-Nev.)	89	Wilson, P. (R-Calif.)	25	Mitchell, G. (D-Maine)	7
Byrd, R. (D-W.Va.)	76	Lugar, R. (R-Ind.)	24	Pryor, D. (D-Ark.)	6

Hatch, O. (R-Utah)	76	Riegle, D. (D-Mich.)	24	Zorinsky, E. (D-Nebr.)	6
Tsongas, P. (D-Mass.)	75	Evans, D. (R-Wash.)	23	Baucus, M. (D-Mont.)	5
Goldwater, B. (R-Ariz.)	57	*Stafford*, R. (R-Vt.)	23	Exon, J. (D-Nebr.)	5
Kasten, R. (R-Wis.)	55	Chafee, J. (R-R.I.)	19	Humphrey, G. (R-N.H.)	5
Nunn, S. (D-Ga.)	55	Danforth, J. (R-Mo.)	19	Boren, D. (D-Okla.)	4
Packwood, B. (R-Oreg.)	52	Durenberger, D. (R-Minn.)	19	Ford, W. (D-Ky.)	4
Metzenbaum, H. (D-Ohio)	47	Bradley, B. (D-N.J.)	19	Heflin, H. (D-Ala.)	4
Hatfield, M. (R-Oreg.)	44	Sarbanes, P. (D-Md.)	19	Mattingly, M. (R-Ga.)	4
Chiles, L. (D-Fla.)	43	*Andrews*, M. (R-N.D.)	18	Trible, P. (R-Va.)	4
Bumpers, D. (D-Ark.)	42	Denton, J. (R-Ala.)	18	Bingaman, J. (D-N.Mex.)	3
Levin, C. (D-Mich.)	41	Proxmire, W. (D-Wis.)	18	Murkowski, F. (R-Alaska)	3
Stevens, T. (R-Alaska)	41	Cohen, W. (R-Maine)	17	Symms, S. (R-Idaho)	3
Weicker, L. (R-Conn.)	41	*Bentsen*, L. (D-Tex.)	16	Nickles, D. (R-Okla.)	2
Armstrong, W. (R-Colo.)	38	Lautenberg, F. (D-N.J.)	16	Burdick, Q. (D-N.D.)	1
D'Amato, A. (R-N.Y.)	34	*Jepsen*, R. (R-Iowa)	15	Hecht, C. (R-Nev.)	1
Biden, J. (D-Del.)	32	Quayle, D. (R-Ind.)	15	Abdnor, J. (R-S.D.)	0
				Dixon, A. (D-Ill.)	0
				Matsunaga, S. (D-Hawaii)	0

a. Senators whose names are italicized held leadership positions in 1983 (see the list of positions in Appendix A). Table italicizes leaders of all standing, special, and select committees of the Senate, and of the Joint Economic Committee. Leaders of the joint committees on Printing, the Library, and Taxation are rarely noted in the media and are not italicized here.

tors are of the most interest to television and newspapers; the same eighty senators are of least interest.

Computations for those at the other end of the scale—the invisible senators—are equally dramatic. Historically the bottom half of the Senate usually accounts for a little more than one-fifth of the senatorial appearances in Associated Press stories. And in the 1983 rating the combined total for the thirty-five senators who received the least attention amounted to 5 percent of the Senate's media score. It is hard to overlook the degree to which most members of the Senate are beyond the interest of the national media, yet it is a phenomenon that has been rarely noted.[6]

During 1983, an ordinary year in the history of the Congress, seventeen senators were never seen on the television news programs that we identify with anchormen Dan Rather, Tom Brokaw, and Peter Jennings; another seventeen were seen once. Thus one-third of the Senate appeared only one time or not at all on the ABC, CBS, and NBC evening news programs combined (1,095 programs). Max Baucus (D-Montana) was seen once on network news asking some questions about the Environmental Protection Agency; Rudy Boschwitz (R-Minnesota) was shown calling for the ouster of Interior Secretary James Watt; the one appearance of Jeremiah Denton (R-Alabama) was a comment on drug trafficking and the Cuban connection; Jake Garn (R-Utah), also seen one time, hoped that President Reagan would veto an excessive budget. Almost half the senators (forty-five) were seen two times or fewer; two-thirds (sixty-five) were on prime-time news programs four times or fewer. Sixty-six senators did not appear on the networks' Sunday interview programs during 1983. The names of five senators never appeared in the index of articles in the *New York Times*, *Washington Post*, *Los Angeles Times*, *Christian Science Monitor*, or *Wall Street Journal*, and two-thirds of all senators were mentioned

6. Among those who have discussed this phenomenon are Eric P. Veblen, "Liberalism and National Newspaper Coverage of Members of Congress," *Polity*, vol. 14 (Fall 1981), p. 154; Doris A. Graber, *Mass Media and American Politics*, 2d ed. (CQ Press, 1984), p. 239; Michael J. Robinson, "Three Faces of Congressional Media," in Thomas E. Mann and Norman J. Ornstein, eds., *The New Congress* (American Enterprise Institute, 1981), p. 87; and Roger H. Davidson and Walter J. Oleszek, *Congress and Its Members*, 2d ed. (CQ Press, 1985), p. 150.

fewer than twenty times in these five major newspapers combined.

On the other hand, in 1983 Howard Baker appeared 45 times and Robert Dole (R-Kansas) 34 times on the nightly news; Daniel P. Moynihan (D-New York) was interviewed 4 times and Christopher Dodd (D-Connecticut) 5 times on the Sunday morning network programs; the five major national papers mentioned Senator John Glenn (D-Ohio) 439 times and Senator Alan Cranston (D-California) 254 times (excluding local stories in the *Los Angeles Times*).

A lot of important television programs reach smaller audiences than the networks' evening news—"Nightline" (ABC), "MacNeil-Lehrer Nightly News Hour" (PBS), "Take Two" (CNN), and the call-in programs on C-SPAN. Do they also concentrate on the same senators? Each afternoon that Congress is in session, Mildred Webber of the Senate Republican Conference staff calls television producers to see what guests will be on their public affairs programs the next day. This information is distributed to Republican senators' offices as "Network Roundup."[7]

Between July 1982 and June 1984 my researchers and I examined 268 days of these compilations, which included 50 separate programs. Senators made 311 appearances. The most often seen, in order, were Dole, Hollings, Hart, Hatch, Dodd, Cranston, Glenn, Baker, and Tsongas. These appearances were primarily on interview programs, as distinct from the networks' daily recitation of the news. Therefore a senator who declined invitations received a lower rating. In 1984, for example, Ted Kennedy apparently had reasons to keep his own counsel because, as press secretary Robert Shrum told me, he had standing invitations from all the Sunday programs. Still, I concluded that these programs do cast their nets wider. Such relatively obscure senators as Arlen Specter (R-Pennsylvania), Larry Pressler (R-South Dakota), and John East (R-

---

7. In a memorandum to Republican senators' press secretaries on August 12, 1982, the Senate Republican Conference wrote that "Network Roundup" serves as a "preview of upcoming public affairs shows, and therefore primarily represents only the advanced scheduled appearances by senators and others, and not always whether they actually appeared. We currently estimate our publication to be accurate approximately 90% of the time."

North Carolina) were likely to be on the air. But in general the programs were most interested in the same senators who scored high in the 1983 ranking and were least interested in the same senators who scored low. Of the 101 senators, 23 were not listed in the "Network Roundup" sample, 29 appeared once, and 13 were seen twice (see appendix table B-11).

What sort of national exposure does the "typical" senator receive on television? By most standards, nothing is typical about John Heinz, whose surname is almost a synonym for ketchup and pickles. By 1983 the handsome, forty-five-year-old Pennsylvania Republican had been twice elected to the Senate after three terms in the House of Representatives. On the networks' evening news programs, Heinz was seen once on CBS (in February, commenting on medicare's responsibility to senior citizens), once on ABC (in September, arguing that the Justice Department had not done enough to protect the U.S. steel industry from Japanese dumping), and twice on NBC (in April and June, both times criticizing the Reagan administration's policy on social security benefits for the mentally disabled). He was also twice noted, but not seen—on CBS (January) as the victim of a post office snafu and on NBC (May) in a story about senators' financial disclosure statements. Out of 1,095 network evening news programs in 1983, Senator Heinz was seen or mentioned six times. Thirty-eight senators received a higher national media ranking and sixty-one ranked lower than he did.

Indicating which senators are leaders is merely one way to divide the members; obviously, not all leadership positions are of equal importance. I am not equating the Finance Committee and the Veterans' Affairs Committee.[8] Moreover, of course, there are 44 leaders in the listing of 101 senators, so the degree to which this suggests a Senate elite must be kept in perspective. But the

8. The Senate divides committees into two categories. The twelve "A" committees are Agriculture, Appropriations, Armed Services, Banking, Commerce, Energy, Environment, Finance, Foreign Relations, Governmental Affairs, Judiciary, and Labor. The seven "B" committees are Budget, Rules, Small Business, Veterans' Affairs, Joint Economic, Aging, and Intelligence. In theory, each Senator is limited to serving on three committees, known as the "two A, one B" rule.

division between so-called leaders and nonleaders does graphically illustrate something about which senators make news:

Top third	Middle third	Bottom third
23 Leaders	15 Leaders	6 Leaders
10 Nonleaders	18 Nonleaders	29 Nonleaders

This is what holding a leadership position has meant to one senator: David Durenberger (R-Minnesota) received eighteen mentions in the 1983 National Newspaper Index; but in 1985, after having become chairman of the Select Committee on Intelligence, his newspaper appearances almost doubled—to thirty-three, of which twenty-six can be attributed directly or indirectly to his new leadership assignment.

Of those who received considerable press attention without benefit of a leadership position in 1983, only one (Howard Metzenbaum) did so by assuming the traditional role of maverick. But, of course, there always will be some mavericks who also hold leadership positions: in 1983, for example, Jesse Helms (chairman of the Agriculture Committee) and William Proxmire (ranking Democrat on the Banking Committee).[9] Donald Riegle (D-Michigan), who switched parties when he was a House member in 1973, said he got more press notice as a maverick Republican than as a mainstream Democrat.

In the game of media attention among junior senators, maverick supersedes mainstream but temporary leader supersedes maverick. An example of the temporary leader—what political scientists would call a coalition leader—is Robert Kasten (R-Wisconsin) who put together a group of senators in March 1983 to successfully oppose

9. James Reston calls Proxmire "one of the Senate's best known mavericks," while Steven Roberts notes that Helms "is seldom interested in the good will of his colleagues or in the legislative achievements that require the patient forging of coalitions and compromises" (characteristics of the mavericks). See "Senator William Proxmire: On the Occasion of a 70th Birthday," New York Times, November 12, 1985; and "Helms Puts in Active Week on His Foreign Policy," New York Times, November 11, 1985. Also see Vermont Royster, "The Mavericks," Wall Street Journal, January 22, 1986.

a withholding tax on savings accounts. Steven V. Roberts noted in the *New York Times* that

> After less than three years in office, [Kasten] picked a major fight with President Reagan and his own party leadership over a new law requiring banks to withhold taxes on interest and dividend payments.
>
> With the aid of the banking industry, the freshman Senator stirred up a tidal wave of protest. Depositors deluged Congress with objections, and the legislators finally capitulated, repealing the law.[10]

Dennis DeConcini (D-Arizona) became a top newsmaker in 1978 when he led the opposition to the Panama Canal Treaty, but in 1983 he was rarely in the news. A junior member with an inclination to be noticed must seek out a pet project, usually some matter within the jurisdiction of a committee on which the senator sits. In 1984, when I was a senator watcher, such situations occurred when Bill Bradley (D-New Jersey) attempted to mobilize support for a tax simplification proposal he called "the fair tax," and Frank Lautenberg (D-New Jersey) tried to get a uniform national drinking age of twenty-one.

Another way of judging why the press chooses to cover certain senators is to examine the ways they are described. My researchers and I went through the *Los Angeles Times* and *USA Today* for six months in 1984, coding 740 descriptions into seven categories. Table 2-3 summarizes our findings.

The slant of coverage seems to be an area in which memory plays funny tricks. Certain types of characterizations have a tendency to stick in our minds—whether because they are so colorful or because they affect our personal biases—and so I might have guessed that press adjectives would have been different than the tabulations of table 2-3. What the table shows, however, is that overwhelmingly reporters merely describe senators in terms of the positions they hold. In part, this finding simply confirms that most of the American media still adheres to the style of "objective" journalism pioneered by the wire services. But identifying senators by their positions also protects the journalist. During the 1973 and 1979 energy crises, for instance, Congress was suddenly

10. "Senate's New Breed Shuns Novice Role," *New York Times*, November 26, 1984.

Table 2-3. *Press Descriptions of U.S. Senators, by Category, 1984*

Category	Percent	Examples
Position	38	Durenberger, a member of the Intelligence Committee. . . . its chairman, Barry Goldwater. . . . Senate Minority Leader Byrd told reporters. . . .
Issue/expertise	19	Proxmire, who awards a Fleece each month for the most wasteful use of the taxpayers' money. . . . Nunn, one of the Senate's most respected voices on military affairs. . . .
Personal characteristic	17	Domenici, quick to blush when complimented and sometimes equally quick to anger. . . . The cool-mannered Colorado senator [Hart], more cerebral than fiesty. . . .
Ideology	9	An arch conservative. . . . Helms is the political leader of the New Right. . . . Perhaps best known for his uncompromising conservatism.
Reputation	9	Cranston, long a powerful member of the Senate. . . . Despite mixed marks from colleagues, Hawkins. . . .
Physical characteristic	4	A tall, slim, bespectacled Westerner . . . Simpson, at 6-foot, 7-inches, the tallest man elected to the Senate. . . .
Previous occupation	4	Moynihan, a former U.S. ambassador to the U.N. and India. . . . Metzenbaum, a self-made millionaire before entering public life. . . .

Sources: For descriptions of Durenberger and Goldwater: *Los Angeles Times*, May 19, 1984; Byrd: USA *Today*, December 12, 1984; Proxmire: USA *Today*, August 13, 1984; Nunn: *Los Angeles Times*, August 11, 1984; Domenici: USA *Today*, August 22, 1984; Hart: *Los Angeles Times*, April 19, 1984; Cranston: *Los Angeles Times*, April 19, 1984; Hawkins: USA *Today*, April 27, 1984; Helms: USA *Today*, June 27, 1984; Simpson: USA *Today*, June 14, 1984; Moynihan: USA *Today*, April 16, 1984; Metzenbaum: USA *Today*, April 27, 1984.

populated by all sorts of energy "experts," so that referring to a senator as a member of the Energy Committee would be one way to assure readers or listeners of the solid basis for the reporters' selections of sources.

There always will be some senators who make news for special reasons that cannot be fitted in a category. In the early 1960s when actor Ronald Reagan was first proposed for governor of California, movie magnate Jack Warner was said to have commented, "No, Jimmy Stewart for Governor—Ronnie for Best Friend."[11] In the 1983 Senate, Paul Laxalt's claim to press attention was "close friend," as in "Senator Paul Laxalt . . . a close friend of the President, denounced the mining."[12]

Only two committees, Foreign Relations and Budget, assured their leading members high media rankings. Eighty-one percent of the score Pete Domenici (R-New Mexico) received from network TV and 79 percent of Charles Percy's score came directly from the chairmanships of these committees; Claiborne Pell (D-Rhode Island) and Lawton Chiles (D-Florida) received 93 percent and 81 percent of their TV points, respectively, for being the senior Democrats on them. Some other senators—Robert Stafford (R-Vermont), Roger Jepsen (R-Iowa), James McClure (R-Idaho), John Heinz (R-Pennsylvania), and Jennings Randolph (D-West Virginia)—would have been ranked considerably lower had they not held leadership positions.

Senators do not automatically make news because of their leadership positions. As noted, Jesse Helms (R-North Carolina) was not judged newsworthy because he was the chairman of the Agriculture Committee. Nor was Daniel P. Moynihan (D-New York) primarily in the news because he was vice-chairman of the Select Committee on Intelligence. Only 5 percent of the appearances by Moynihan on the network evening news can be attributed to that post, and only once in 1983 was Helms mentioned because of his Agriculture chairmanship.

No senator can be forced to appear before the cameras: the real

11. Stephen Hess and David S. Broder, *The Republican Establishment* (Harper & Row, 1967), p. 243.

12. Doyle McManus, "Covert War—A Strategy Backfires," *Los Angeles Times*, April 13, 1984.

anomaly of these data is that Robert Byrd, the minority leader, ranks seventeenth in national media exposure during 1983. No other minority leader was lower than sixth in the previous thirty years, and one, Everett Dirksen (R-Illinois), was even ranked first in the Eighty-ninth Congress. "I'm not just a pretty face," said the stocky, sixty-seven-year-old Byrd in a moment of uncharacteristic humor.[13] The West Virginian, in fact, has tried to use his aversion to TV interviews to undergird his leadership position by putting forward other Democrats as party spokesmen. After Byrd had been reelected Democratic leader in December 1984, Bill Bradley said that he had "done a good job of sharing the spotlight with a lot of different senators. People [read Democratic senators] understand and appreciate that."[14] (However, the 1984 challenge to Byrd's Democratic leadership, combined with the more aggressive style of the new Republican leader, Bob Dole, apparently has produced a change in the senator. According to a May 8, 1985, report by Jonathan Fuerbringer, Byrd had "talked to the press more in the last three weeks than perhaps in all the previous 12 months.")[15]

Still, the fact that senators hold leadership positions *and* make news means that the national media—for whatever reasons—accurately reflect the power structure of the Senate within certain limits.

It has been assumed that when television came of age—network news expanded from fifteen minutes to a half hour in 1963—the younger (presumably junior) members of Congress would be the most skilled at exploiting the expanded coverage because they were more comfortable with the medium. Yet national coverage over the past three decades has become increasingly dominated by the senior (presumably older) members in leadership positions.

In 1953–54 (the Eighty-third Congress) the Republicans were the majority party in the Senate; Joseph R. McCarthy (R-Wiscon-

13. Helen Dewar, "Byrd Reelected Minority Leader of the Senate," *Washington Post*, December 13, 1985.

14. Steven V. Roberts, "Byrd Reelected Minority Leader," *New York Times*, December 13, 1984.

15. "Byrd: No More Mr. Quiet Guy," *New York Times*, May 9, 1985.

sin), chairman of the Government Operations Committee, was making headlines investigating communist influence in the army; and William Knowland (R-California) was the majority leader and Lyndon B. Johnson (D-Texas) was the minority leader. As indicated in the appendix tables, McCarthy (1), Knowland (2), and Johnson (6) were among the Senate's top twenty newsmakers in terms of Associated Press appearances, along with the chairmen of Judiciary (William Langer, R-North Dakota), Republican Policy (Homer Ferguson, R-Michigan), Banking (Homer Capehart, R-Indiana), Interstate and Foreign Commerce (John Bricker, R-Ohio), the Joint Committee on Reduction of Nonessential Federal Expenditures (Harry F. Byrd, Sr., D-Virginia), Armed Services (Leverett Saltonstall, R-Massachusetts), and the Democratic Campaign Committee (first-termer Albert Gore, Sr., D-Tennessee). The other half of the top twenty did not hold leadership positions: Wayne Morse (I-Oregon), Estes Kefauver (D-Tennessee), Hubert Humphrey (D-Minnesota), Clinton Anderson (D-New Mexico), Paul Douglas (D-Illinois), Irving Ives (R-New York), Herbert Lehman (D-New York), John Sherman Cooper (R-Kentucky), John Sparkman (D-Alabama), and Thomas Hennings (D-Missouri).

The Eighty-ninth Congress (1965–66), the next Congress examined, was controlled by the Democrats. Mike Mansfield (D-Montana) was majority leader and Everett Dirksen (R-Illinois) minority leader. Once again the top twenty newsmakers were divided evenly between leaders and nonleaders. Those without leadership positions were Robert Kennedy (D-New York), Paul Douglas (D-Illinois), Thomas Dodd (D-Connecticut), Edward Kennedy (D-Massachusetts), John Tower (R-Texas), Wayne Morse (D-Oregon), Hugh Scott (R-Pennsylvania), Joseph Clark (D-Pennsylvania), Strom Thurmond (R-South Carolina), and John Stennis (D-Mississippi). In 1969–70 there were eleven leaders and nine nonleaders; in 1973–74, fourteen leaders and six nonleaders. Of those mentioned most often on the network evening news in 1981–82, seventeen were leaders and three were nonleaders; in the 1983 national media ranking only four of the top twenty senators were nonleaders.

Thus the decline of the nonleader as a newsmaker has been precipitous, from 50 percent of this elite in the 1950s and 1960s, and 30 percent in 1973–74, to 15–20 percent by the 1980s.

It should be noted, however, that 6 percent more Senate members qualify as leaders in 1983 than in 1953 and 1964 (using the same definition of leadership in all Congresses). Mostly this is because senators in the earlier Congresses had more than one leadership position. In 1964, for example, Senator Saltonstall was the ranking Republican on three committees (Appropriations, Armed Services, and Small Business).

Still, the trend line is in exactly the opposite direction from what had been expected. Why? One speculation is that senators have changed.

Many of the Senate's nonleaders who made news in the 1950s and 1960s did so for reasons that are always sufficient, of course: Estes Kefauver was a potential presidential nominee, Thomas Dodd was involved in a scandal, Wayne Morse and Strom Thurmond switched parties, Irving Ives and John Sherman Cooper lost elections of more than routine interest because of their opponents (Averell Harriman and Alben Barkley, respectively). John Sparkman, a low-profile senator, had a temporary burst of press attention when he was chosen Democratic vice-presidential candidate in 1952. And Wayne Morse set a Senate filibuster record by holding the floor twenty-two hours and twenty-six minutes in 1953.

At the same time, lawmakers who were often seen and heard in 1953–54 without benefit of a leadership position were not always new to public life. Herbert Lehman, for example, was a freshman senator, but he was also a four-time governor of New York; Clinton Anderson, another freshman, had been secretary of agriculture; Hubert Humphrey, who had led the fight for a strong civil rights plank in the 1948 Democratic platform, entered the Senate as a hero of the liberal movement. Much the same analysis applies to the 1965–66 Congress with such highly visible senators as Robert Kennedy (former attorney general) and Hugh Scott (former chairman of the Republican National Committee). Important, perhaps, in describing this change is that in 1953–54 thirty senators had been governors of their states; by 1983–84 there were only twelve ex-governors in the Senate.[16] About the same number of

16. Everything in politics is subject to change, however. Reporting from the annual meeting of the National Governors Association in 1984, David S. Broder

senators had been members of the House of Representatives in both periods—thirty-six in 1953–54 and thirty-two in 1983–84—but eighteen of the 1953–54 senators had served in the House for five or more terms; only six senators had done so in 1983–84. In other words, thirty years ago, newcomers tended to bring greater reputations to the Senate than junior senators now do and may have been judged more newsworthy by the Washington press corps. Of his Senate colleagues in 1985, John C. Stennis (D-Mississippi), a senator for thirty-eight years, mused, "I am not blaming them. They come here on the average well educated. But they don't have the maturity, if I may use that term. They don't have the experience in public affairs that the old-timer had."[17] It is an observation that scholars have empirically confirmed.[18]

Much has been made of the fact that junior senators—like well-brought-up children—were once expected to be seen and not heard. The folkway of serving an apprenticeship in the 1950s was "the first rule of Senate behavior," according to Donald R. Matthews: "the new senator [was] expected to keep his mouth shut, not to take the lead in floor fights, to listen and to learn."[19] Yet ironically in 1953–54 a group of vocal first-termers, including Hubert Humphrey, Paul Douglas, Albert Gore, and Thomas Hennings, led the opposition to the Eisenhower administration. It is not unreasonable to conclude that these junior senators got more attention than did junior senators thirty years later because

commented, "From the talk at this conference, there may be a mass movement of governors into national politics, via the Senate races. . . . At least eight governors, and perhaps as many as a dozen, are considered potential candidates for the Senate in 1986, and most of them are expected to be very competitive contenders if they run." See "Governors Eyeing Senate Seats," Columbia (S.C.) State, August 1, 1984.

17. Steven V. Roberts, "Senator John C. Stennis: Wisdom in Judgment, 38 Years in the Making," New York Times, November 4, 1985.

18. Dennis M. Simon and David T. Canon, "Actors, Athletes, and Astronauts: Amateurism and Changing Career Paths in the United States Senate," paper prepared for the 1984 annual meeting of the Midwest Political Science Association. See table 6, p. 35, which shows that from 1944 to 1952, 16.9 percent of senators had "no elective experience" before serving in the Senate and that this percentage rose to 32.4 between 1974 and 1982; the comparable figures for "no public experience" were 6.0 from 1944 to 1952 and 14.1 from 1974 to 1982.

19. U.S. Senators & Their World (Vintage, 1960), pp. 92–93.

they deserved more attention. The odd fact that junior senators were more visible in the national media in 1953 than in 1983 might be particularly interesting to today's political scientists who conclude that the "norm of apprenticeship" no longer exists in the Senate.[20]

(I am not contending here that the calibre of the Senate has declined. Warren Cikins, who served on congressional staffs in the 1950s and 1960s, argues that there is no senator today as stupid as George "Molly" Malone, Nevada Republican (1947–59), while Senator Stennis told me that they no longer mint senators of the quality of Eugene Millikin, Colorado Republican (1941–57). A combined Cikins-Stennis theory might be that today's Senate has shaved the peaks and valleys of past performance—less brilliance but less ineptness. In support of this notion, perhaps, are the responses to a question I often asked senators in 1984: "If you could pick the word that reporters put before your name, what would it be?" Most often mentioned was "hard-working," as in hard-working John Melcher (D-Montana) or hard-working Slade Gorton (R-Washington). A senator who most wishes to be remembered as hard-working is not likely to be especially colorful.)[21]

The 1950s were still in the era of the Senate's inner club and one gets the impression from William S. White's Citadel, published in 1957, that the Senate leadership—except for the majority leader and the minority leader—found it just a bit unseemly to be too prominently featured in the press. Many of those whom White identifies as members of the outer club—Lehman, Kefauver, Ferguson, Douglas, Morse, McCarthy—were often in the headlines. (White, the New York Times Senate correspondent, reports this with apparent disdain, as if he agrees that making news is not quite gentlemanly.) On the other hand, the bottom half of the 1953–54 Associated Press appearances list is filled with inner clubbers such

20. See David W. Rohde, Norman J. Ornstein, and Robert L. Peabody, "Political Change and Legislative Norms in the U.S. Senate, 1957–1974," in Glenn R. Parker, ed., Studies of Congress (CQ Press, 1985), p. 179.

21. Strangely, "hard-working" showed up only once in my collection of newspaper adjectives. James McClure (R-Idaho) was called "earnest, hard-working, reliable" by the National Review, October 5, 1984.

as Theodore Francis Green, Frank Carlson, Carl Hayden, and Frederick Payne.[22]

Another reason that today's younger and junior senators have not turned into instant stars may be that being attracted to and skilled at television appearances is not as generational as commentators assumed. The evidence is that senators' media ratings rise as they grow older and gain seniority.

Senators' place in 1983 ranking	Average age	Average number of years in Senate
Top ten	57.6	13.2
Top third	55.6	12.7
Middle third	54.7	8.9
Bottom third	53.2	7.3

Still, Paul Duke, host of "Washington Week in Review" on PBS, was just one of the newsmen who told me that there is now a new breed of young senators who answer reporters' questions in "thirty second bites." He contrasted the newcomers with Jacob Javits, the New York Republican, who "couldn't keep an answer under five minutes." Mark Goodin, the Judiciary Committee's press secretary, says that Chairman Strom Thurmond, eighty years old in 1983, is "one of those old-fashioned orators who works his way up to making a point." Indeed, some will never excel at the pithy responses that TV news broadcasters feel they need. But not every long-winded orator is going to be an octogenarian.

Jerry Woodruff, press secretary to first-term Senator John East, says that he has often urged his boss to keep his answers short, "but as a former professor he thinks in forty-minute bites." Marion Getz, a TV producer for the Democratic Policy Committee, tells of an ill-at-ease young senator who gave a fifty-five second statement for the cameras without blinking. She jokes that it is hard not to blink for almost a minute.

The generational difference that Paul Duke and others refer to may have more to do with when a person was first elected to the Senate than with a senator's age. Older senators who have been

22. See Citadel: The Story of the U.S. Senate (Harper, 1957), especially chapter 7.

elected since the coming of the television era may be more at-
tuned to the needs of the medium than senators (now getting on
in years) who were elected before television became the dominant
force in politics.

Statistically, however, the senators most sought after by national reporters are fast approaching sixty years of age and are in
their third term—unless, of course, a senator is seeking the presidency, in which case the news media are interested regardless of
age or leadership position.

III

The Right Committees

PERHAPS AN APPROPRIATE MOTTO to place on the desk of an ambitious legislator would be *Where You Sit Determines How Often You Will Be Photographed*. It makes a difference whether one sits on the majority or minority side of the aisle in the Senate chamber, as we shall see.[1] And the congressional committees a legislator sits on are even more important. Getting on the right committees is the threshold that a senator must cross in order to be recognized by Washington journalists. The right committees do not guarantee success, but being on the wrong committees is the high road to going nowhere in the news media.

The Foreign Relations Committee, for instance, may no longer be the crown jewel of Senate committees or "the repository of considerable foreign affairs expertise and experience" (Leslie H. Gelb), and it may have "seen most of its power and prestige slowly dribble away in recent years" (*Congressional Quarterly*), but these are assessments of the cognoscenti who view Congress through a kaleidoscope of constantly shifting patterns.[2] For most of the national media, the Foreign Relations Committee, as its name

1. See pp. 56–57.
2. Leslie H. Gelb, "For Senate Foreign Relations Panel, More Partisanship and Less Influence," *New York Times*, November 27, 1984; and "Majority Leader Vote Fallout Affects Three Senate Panels," *Congressional Quarterly Weekly Report*, vol. 42 (December 1, 1984), p. 3026.

implies, is the locus of congressional activity in the area that Washington journalism finds most newsworthy.[3] Nor is this just because of the importance given to international relations: there is also the spice of what Murrey Marder sees as Congress's "surge of assertiveness in foreign policy."[4] While sixteen of nineteen Senate committees have "some jurisdiction over foreign policy" according to one study,[5] when the three television networks focus on a committee hearing, the committee they are covering—overwhelmingly—is Foreign Relations.

The next best place for a senator to be noticed is in a seat at a Judiciary Committee hearing. In recent years, Judiciary has repeatedly made news because of its jurisdiction over civil rights bills, anticrime legislation (including such questions as the death penalty and the insanity defense), proposed constitutional amendments (the equal rights amendment, school prayer, attempts to overturn the Supreme Court's 1973 decision legalizing abortion), and immigration reform, as well as confirmation hearings on several controversial nominations to the Supreme Court. The fastest rising seat of influence in terms of media attention—now in third place—is the Budget Committee, followed by a perennial favorite of the press corps, the Governmental Affairs Committee, once known as Government Operations, which has broad authority to investigate (but not legislate) and is therefore especially involved in finding waste and malfeasance in the president's agencies.

Adding up the number of ABC, CBS, and NBC cameras that were in committee hearing rooms from February 1979 through June 1984 makes clear where a senator should be in order to be seen on the evening news (see table 3-1).[6]

3. See Stephen Hess, *The Washington Reporters* (Brookings, 1981), p. 109.

4. "Hill Fights Reagan for Soul of Foreign Policy," *Washington Post*, September 2, 1984.

5. See Lee H. Hamilton and Michael H. Van Dusen, "Making the Separation of Powers Work," *Foreign Affairs*, vol. 57 (Summer 1979), p. 31.

6. Having cameras at a hearing does not ensure that a story will be on the air, of course. Often one network does not expect to do a story but sends a crew to protect itself in case a rival decides to use a piece on a hearing. Then, too, a story is sometimes dropped at the last minute to make room for late-breaking events. However, the primacy of Foreign Relations and Judiciary (although not Governmental Affairs) also can be seen in data compiled by Steven S. Smith and Christo-

Table 3-1. Ranking of Senate Committees by Number of Network Television Cameras Covering Them

Committee	Number of cameras[a]
Foreign Relations	522
Judiciary	252
Budget	156
Governmental Affairs	152
Appropriations	141
Labor and Human Resources	134
Joint Economic	133
Armed Services	131
Energy and Natural Resources	120
Finance	98
Banking, Housing, and Urban Affairs	97
Ethics	82
Commerce, Science, and Transportation	61
Environment and Public Works	60
Agriculture, Nutrition, and Forestry	43
Aging	23
Intelligence	22
Rules and Administration	20
Small Business	6
Veterans' Affairs	1
Indian Affairs	0

a. This data is collected by Lawrence Janezich, the principal deputy to Max Barber, superintendent of the Senate radio and television gallery. With the permission of Mr. Barber, when senators and reporters were at the Democratic and Republican conventions during the summer of 1984, my three interns—Stephen Davis, Janet Hatfield, and Nancy Kates—moved into the television gallery and meticulously copied Janezich's worksheets, which then covered over 2,000 committee hearings using over 6,500 cameras and 5,000 radio microphones.

A five-and-a-half year compilation of committee hearings does not necessarily reflect an even flow of attention from the networks: seventy-four cameras covered Energy Committee meetings during the oil crisis in 1979; more than half of the cameras that came to the Rules Committees were there in 1981 (the issue was whether there should be television coverage of the Senate floor);

---

pher J. Deering, who counted the minutes of the "CBS Evening News" devoted to topics falling within the jurisdictions of congressional committees (1975–80 sample). They found that over 50 percent of their tabulation for the Senate came from the two top committees. See *Committees in Congress* (CQ Press, 1984), p. 67.

all of the Ethics Committee's cameras focused on two cases involving Senators Herman Talmadge (1979) and Harrison Williams (1980–81). Special attention was paid to the Environment Committee in 1979 (Three Mile Island), the Judiciary Committee in 1980 ("Billygate," the activities of President Carter's brother), and the Banking Committee in 1980 (Federal loans to New York City and Chrysler Corporation, as well as the Soviet grain embargo). Importantly, the figures understate the present popularity of the Budget Committee, which was created in 1974, and was barely noticed by the cameras until 1981.

It is typical of Washington news coverage that the focus of television and print reporters is not very different. Looking at four newspapers—the *Washington Post, Los Angeles Times, Chicago Tribune,* and *New Orleans Times-Picayune*—Susan Heilmann Miller found that in 1973–74 there were substantially more stories about Foreign Relations and Judiciary than the other standing committees.[7] One of the reasons for the lopsided coverage in both print and visual media, of course, is that national news organizations do not keep enough reporters permanently assigned to the Congress to cover all hearings. On seven days in May 1984, I watched the AP's Tom Raum allocate his bureau's resources. The Senate held sixty hearings in this period and the AP covered 65 percent of them. On a quiet Monday or Friday all hearings were covered. But in midweek—Wednesday, May 23, for example—reporters were assigned to only six of fifteen Senate committee hearings (and six of twenty-two House committee hearings).[8]

7. See "Congress and the News Media: Coverage, Collaboration and Agenda-Setting" (Ph.D. dissertation, Stanford University, 1976), p. 24. Miller's survey covered October 1973 to March 1974. The Watergate hearings, conducted by Senator Ervin's Select Committee on Presidential Campaign Activities, led the list (2,430 stories), but among the standing committees the coverage was Foreign Relations (808 stories), Judiciary (791), Commerce (444), Armed Services (413), Government Operations (404), Banking (344), Appropriations (279), Finance (262), Labor (250), Interior (249), and Rules (242). Changes in Senate committees, which took effect in 1977, make comparisons with 1983–84 only approximate.

8. The AP covered thirty-nine Senate hearings and thirty-eight House hearings. But it covered only 34 percent of the House hearings, which reinforces a point made in *The Washington Reporters*, p. 106, that the House has to work twice as hard as the Senate in order to equal the media's attention paid to the latter. Also Tom Raum notes that the percentage of committees covered would be even less in the

When the media rankings of senators are grouped by their committees, a clear pattern emerges, one that closely parallels a typology devised by Steven S. Smith and Christopher J. Deering.[9] Senators on policy committees make the most national news, followed by senators on mixed policy/constituency committees; the least national news comes from the group of senators who are on the purely constituency committees (see table 3-2).

A self-selection process partly accounts for which senators serve on which committees. As senators gain seniority they can bargain for more desirable assignments, with full knowledge of which committees translate into the most media potential. A senator who aspires to be the chairman of Environment and Public Works (formerly the Public Works Committee) will have considerable power within the Senate but few mentions on network television news. (Edward Martin ranked eighty-fifth in 1953–54, Jennings Randolph was eighty–second in 1973–74, and Robert Stafford was fifty-third in 1983.) As Joseph Nocera wrote in 1978,

> Jennings Randolph, whatever his other virtues, is never going to have what it takes to get great press. . . . Chairman of the Public Works Committee is the powerful post Randolph holds in the Senate. He is a master grantsman for West Virginia, creating dams where there was only river. . . . To get great press you have to create *news*, and that's a different matter entirely. None of this quiet, behind-the-scenes stuff that Jennings Randolph prefers.[10]

A senator's committees will often define what he wants from public life. When Bob Dole switched from Agriculture to Finance—a move that was not popular with Kansas farmers—he could expect to be more nationally newsworthy. Or take the case of Washington's Daniel Evans, who was appointed and then elected to the Senate in 1983 and ranked one hundredth in seniority in 1984. The freshman senator was assigned to two of the less-noticed committees, Environment and Public Works and Energy and Natural Resources (the latter, however, was particularly

---

first session of a Congress: by May 1984 much of the major legislation already had been reported out of committee.

9. See *Committees in Congress*, pp. 113–17.

10. "How to Make the Front Page," *Washington Monthly* (October 1978), pp. 12–13.

Table 3-2. *Ranking of Senate Committees by Amount of Media Attention,*
Average, 1953-83

Committee	1953-83 Ranking [a]	Type
Foreign Relations	1.8	Policy
Judiciary	2.6	Policy
Budget	3.0 (1983 only)	Policy
Governmental Affairs	5.0	Policy
Armed Services	6.0	Policy/constituency
Labor	6.8	Policy
Banking	7.2	Policy/constituency
Appropriations	8.2	Constituency
Finance	9.0	Policy/constituency
Commerce	10.6	Constituency
Agriculture	11.2	Constituency
Energy	12.0 (1983 only)	Constituency
Environment	13.8	Constituency
Small Business	15.0 (1983 only)	Constituency
Veterans' Affairs	15.0 (1973-74, 1983 only)	Constituency

a. These figures reflect an average of the collective rankings of the members of
each committee for the years 1953-54, 1965-66, 1969-70, 1973-74, and 1983. For
example, the members of the Foreign Relations Committee ranked 1 (1953-54), 3
(1965-66), 2 (1969-70), 2 (1973-74), and 1 (1983) for an average of 1.8.

important to his state). Evans's background suggests that he will
not remain a low-profile senator. He comes from a state that has
been noted for highly visible legislators in recent years, and he is a
former three-term governor, a former college president, and was
the keynote speaker at a Republican presidential convention. By
1985, when he outranked seven other senators, Evans left the
Environment and Public Works Committee, retained membership
on Energy and Natural Resources, and joined the Foreign Relations Committee.

Some of the attention given to the Foreign Relations Committee is attention given to senators who see themselves as future
presidents. No other committee can rival Foreign Relations as the
incubator of presidential contenders. This elite group since 1953
has included Robert A. Taft, William Knowland, Hubert Hum-

phrey, John Kennedy, Frank Church, Stuart Symington, Eugene McCarthy, Edmund Muskie, George McGovern, Howard Baker, John Glenn, and Alan Cranston.[11] One need not state this as a chicken-or-egg proposition: the Foreign Relations Committee has as magnetic an effect on the media as has the White House for senators.[12]

When a committee makes news its members make news:

PENTAGON LISTS BUDGET CUTS
by Rick Atkinson and Walter Pincus
Washington Post, May 4, 1984

In testimony before the Senate Armed Services Committee, [Defense Secretary] Weinberger made no effort to hide his regret at the cuts, and when Sen. J. James Exon (D-Nebraska) asked where further cuts could be made. . . .

But Sen. Carl Levin (D-Michigan) told Weinberger, "You come up here saying every year that if we cut one dollar. . . .

Sen. Sam Nunn (D-Georgia), a Senate leader on defense matters, pulled him up short on that issue. . . .

Sen. John W. Warner (R-Virginia), a former Navy secretary, questioned the cut of an attack submarine. . . .

This hearing was also covered by ABC, CBS, NBC, CNN, and C-SPAN. Despite insiders' talk of which committees are in and which are in decline, the general outline of where news is made has not changed over the past three decades.

Most senators now serve on three or four committees, but some have more high-publicity assignments than others. When I asked Delaware Senator Joseph Biden what he felt accounted for his newsworthiness, he replied without hesitation, "It's the committees, of course." In 1983–84 Biden was a member of the three most televised committees—Foreign Relations, Judiciary (where he was the ranking Democrat), and Budget, as well as the Select Committee on Intelligence; Orrin Hatch was chairman of Labor, chairman of the Constitution Subcommittee of Judiciary (with jurisdiction over such matters as the equal rights amendment), and served on Budget; Howard Metzenbaum's committees were Bud-

11. Having apparently been forced to abandon presidential aspirations, Glenn switched from Foreign Relations to the Armed Services Committee in 1985.

12. See Richard F. Fenno, Jr., *Congressmen in Committees* (Little Brown, 1973), pp. 141–42.

get, Energy, Judiciary, and Labor; Charles Grassley had seats on Budget, Finance, Judiciary, and Labor; and Charles Mathias was on Rules (chairman), Foreign Relations, Governmental Affairs, and Judiciary.[13] At the other extreme, some senators did not sit on any of the committees that ranked among the top eight on the scale of network coverage, including David Boren (D-Oklahoma), Alan Dixon (D-Illinois), Wendell Ford (D-Kentucky), Chic Hecht (R-Nevada), Frank Lautenberg (D-New Jersey), John Melcher (D-Montana), George Mitchell (D-Maine), David Pryor (D-Arkansas), and Malcolm Wallop (R-Wyoming).[14]

In his portrait of the Senate in the 1950s, Donald Matthews wrote that a senator was expected "to focus his energy and attention on the relatively few matters that come before his committees. . . ."[15] More recently, however, political scientists of the 1970s and 1980s have described a Senate moving away from specialization. The need to be able to answer whatever questions television reporters might have on their minds has been given as one of the reasons behind the new-style generalists.[16] Yet as the data in this study illustrate, national reporters continue to seek out interviewees from the appropriate committees, the experts-cum-insiders. The national media need specialists; when they choose which senator to interview, it is often exactly because the senator can be counted on to be recognized as an expert.

The reason committees were originally expected to be the keystone of television coverage was that they are where Congress performs its oversight function. Indeed, Senate investigations,

13. Other senators who benefited from media-attracting committee assignments were Nancy Kassebaum (Budget, Commerce, Foreign Relations), Robert Kasten (Appropriations, Budget, Commerce), Dan Quayle (Armed Services, Budget, Labor), Donald Riegle (Banking, Budget, Commerce, Labor), and Steve Symms (Budget, Environment, Finance, Joint Economic).

14. However, in the Ninety-ninth Congress (1985–86), several of these senators improved their committee assignments: Dixon joined the Armed Services Committee; Wallop became a member of the Labor Committee; and, most important in terms of upward mobility, Lautenberg went from Banking and Commerce to Appropriations, Budget, and Environment.

15. U.S. *Senators & Their World* (Vintage, 1960), p. 95.

16. See David W. Rohde, Norman J. Ornstein, and Robert L. Peabody, "Political Change and Legislative Norms in the U.S. Senate, 1957–1974," in Glenn R. Parker, ed., *Studies of Congress* (CQ Press, 1985), p. 178.

sometimes conducted by a special or select committee, have produced a number of television's great moments. Estes Kefauver's
1951 chairmanship of hearings on organized crime catapulted him
into national prominence. The Crime Committee won an Emmy in
1952 and Kefauver won fourteen of the sixteen state primaries
before losing the Democratic presidential nomination to Adlai
Stevenson.[17] The Army-McCarthy hearings were the riveting
drama of the 1954 television season and led to Joseph McCarthy's
censure by the Senate. Chairman John McClellan's examination of
labor racketeering, with Robert F. Kennedy as chief counsel, was
well covered between 1957 and 1959.

Such presentations, especially coming in the formative period
of television as the national medium, led to forecasts that the
huge potential for publicity would transform senatorial committee
rooms into home-screen circuses. This has happened, but primarily in exceptional circumstances. Commercial networks devoted
approximately 235 hours of live coverage to the Watergate hearings during the summer of 1973. Viewers in over 47 million homes
became fascinated by the personalities of the senators doing the
questioning—Chairman Sam Ervin (D-North Carolina), Vice-
Chairman Howard Baker (R-Tennessee), Herman Talmadge (D-
Georgia), Edward Gurney (R-Florida), Daniel Inouye (D-Hawaii),
Lowell Weicker (R-Connecticut), and Joseph Montoya (D-New
Mexico). Baker even suddenly pulled ahead of Edward Kennedy in
a Harris poll trial heat for president.[18]

As *Congressional Quarterly* notes, congressional investigations
have "tranformed minor politicians into household words."[19]
What is probably more interesting, however, given our expecta-
tions, is how seldom this has happened in recent years. Indeed,
looking back on such earlier investigators as Gerald Nye and Harry
Truman, Senate oversight hearings may not even have produced
as many stars as in the era before television.

17. See Ron Garay, "Television and the 1951 Senate Crime Committee Hearings," *Journal of Broadcasting*, vol. 22 (Fall 1978), pp. 484–85.
18. See Michael J. Robinson, "The Impact of the Televised Watergate Hearings," *Journal of Communication*, vol. 24 (Spring 1974), p. 17; and Robert Walters,
"The Howard Baker Boom," *Columbia Journalism Review*, vol. 12 (November/Decem-
ber 1973), pp. 33–37.
19. *Congressional Quarterly's Guide to Congress*, 3d ed. (CQ Press, 1982), p. 161.

Occasionally a legislator takes charge of an issue—from the journalists' perspective—without benefit of the appropriate committee assignment or without sufficient time in service or both. (Jack Kemp, a member of the House of Representatives, who successfully staked a claim to being Mr. Supply-Side Economics in Congress, is an obvious example of this phenomenon.)

A legislator can acquire such squatters' rights to an issue because of a *vacuum* (the natural leader declines to come forward); *expertise* (enough knowledge to impress the press corps); *timing* (early recognition of the issue's news value); *publicity skills* (scaring off equally legitimate competitors by calling attention to one's claim); and *good luck* (picking an issue that circumstances elevate to the front page).

Unlike having a temporary leadership position, in which a legislator steps forward as the chief proponent or opponent of a specific bill, going after squatters' rights is an attempt to take permanent possession of an entire subject area. Senator Dan Quayle's press secretary, Peter Lincoln, told me in 1984 that his boss was "trying to educate himself on health matters. I'll put out a piece of paper [press release] on a health issue, even though I don't expect it to get into print, so that reporters will eventually make the connection 'Quayle-health.' "

Sam Nunn, who probably will be the chairman of the Armed Services Committee when the Democrats next control the Senate, was the most junior member of the committee in 1973 when he began to establish squatters' rights over NATO policy questions. Elected in 1972 at the age of thirty-four, in his first year in the Senate he coauthored an amendment to the Military Procurement Act that required U.S. troops to be withdrawn from Europe in proportion to the balance-of-payments deficit resulting from maintaining them there.[20] And by the next year, John W. Finney was reporting in the *New York Times* that

20. John W. Finney, "Senate Clause Is Used to Prod NATO on Troop Costs," *New York Times*, November 24, 1973. In 1984 Nunn, now the most influential Democrat on the committee, offered virtually the same amendment; although he lost in the Senate, other NATO nations pledged to increase their financial commitments. See James R. Dickenson, "Newly Assertive Sen. Nunn Leads the Offense on Defense," *Washington Post*, October 17, 1985.

Senator Nunn, the junior member of the Senate Armed Services Committee, was instructed earlier this year by Senator John C. Stennis, the committee chairman, to undertake a study of American troop commitments in Europe.

The 35-year-old Senator's study constitutes the first serious challenge from a member of the pro-Pentagon committee to the Defense Department's long-held planning assumption that a relatively long war would be fought in Europe, with the United States shipping over large numbers of divisions as it did in World War II.

In a committee dominated by older members whose military thinking was largely shaped by World War II, this assumption has tended to be accepted by the majority. Now it is being challenged by a member who was 7 years old when World War II ended and who is emerging as the military expert among the new generation entering the Senate.[21]

Wall Street Journal reporter David Shribman has traced the evolution of John Danforth (R-Missouri) "from a bland Midwestern Republican who made only small ripples in the Senate into a symbol of the new concern over America's trade posture."[22] In 1977 Danforth saw a problem area ("earlier than most") and turned himself into an expert ("through reading, constant exchanges of memorandums and long, late-afternoon Socratic meetings.") When the Republicans gained control of the Senate in 1981, Danforth was able to become chairman of its trade subcommittee; his tight reelection campaign in 1982 convinced him of the political necessity to speak more forcefully. "Before that race," he says, "I was much more pastel, much less vivid than I think I am now." So by the spring of 1985, when his resolution calling for immediate U.S. action if Japan refused to open its markets passed the Senate on a 92-0 vote, John Danforth had become the legislator reporters wanted to quote when writing stories about protectionism and international trade.

Even more dramatic is the squatters' rights claimed in the Senate by Christopher Dodd on the issue of U.S. policy toward Central America. This is the example of a junior Democratic senator be-

---

21. "Pentagon Thesis Disputed in Study," *New York Times*, April 9, 1974.

22. See "Sen. Danforth Battles for Trade Reprisals, Fears 'Real' Protection," *Wall Street Journal*, December 2, 1985.

coming the leading opponent of an increasingly important segment of President Reagan's foreign policy, thereby rising to fifteenth place in the 1983 national media ranking, the highest mark
achieved by a freshman.

Dodd was elected to the Senate in 1980 after serving three
terms in the House of Representatives, where his committees had
been Judiciary and Rules and his interests were largely domestic.
As a senator he won assignment to the Foreign Relations Committee, but he ranked last in seniority, below Pell, Biden, Glenn,
Sarbanes, Zorinsky, Tsongas, and Cranston. He was also the low-
est-ranked Democrat on the Western Hemisphere Affairs Subcommittee, after Zorinsky, Tsongas, and Cranston, although subcommittees are not as important on Foreign Relations as on other
standing committees. Zorinsky was not a serious newsmaker,
Tsongas was most interested in Africa (and also had cancer), Cranston was most interested in arms control (and was running for a
presidential nomination). Dodd, who had been a Peace Corps
volunteer in the Dominican Republic and was fluent in Spanish,
was genuinely interested in the region and anxious to fill the
vacuum.

After less than six months, Dodd earned his first Senate victory,
an amendment to the foreign aid authorization bill requiring that
continued aid to El Salvador depend on a semiannual certification
by the president that "significant progress" is being made to
implement economic, political, and human rights changes. Dodd's
initiative included frequent trips to Central America. After each
visit he reported his impressions as a guest on one of the key
Sunday interview programs, and these were then duly noted in
the newspapers, which increasingly rely on television to make
Monday morning news for them. "I know how [to get on the air],"
Dodd told Greg Schneiders. "I think in 20-second clips."[23] There
were also op-ed page articles and a blizzard of press releases to
remind journalists of the initiator's expertise.

The big breakthrough for Dodd came in April 1983 when Presi-

23. "The 90-Second Handicap," *Washington Journalism Review*, vol. 6 (June 1985),
p. 46.

dent Reagan used a joint session of Congress as the platform to promote his Latin American aid program. It was the Senate's turn to reply, and Minority Leader Byrd chose the Connecticut Senator to give the Democrats' response, ten minutes on all three networks immediately following the president. According to David S. Broder, "Dodd rejected what he called [the] 'legalistic approach' and framed his reply as a broad and emotional indictment of those who would 'loose the dogs of war' on a region whose real problems, he said, are economic and social, not ideological."[24] It was a controversial performance. The *New York Times*, for example, devoted a full column to Jeane Kirkpatrick's response to Dodd. (She called Dodd "demogogic" and "irresponsible.")[25] And by July the "Style" section of the *Washington Post* was telling its readers that the thirty-nine-year-old divorced Senator dated Bianca Jagger and that "his speech made the kind of splash that a young, ambitious senator dreams of—not least because he, like most of them, thinks that someday he might like to be president."[26]

Making news from Washington—at least in the national media—involves, as Christopher Dodd's Senate career to date illustrates, the desire to make news, a talent for making news, a "product" in the form of information or expertise that is superior to what competitors are peddling, and knowledge in an area that journalists think is important or else in an area that is of immediate interest because of events that are beyond the control of the Congress and its members. Membership on the right committees in the Senate will remain the basis for becoming a congressional newsmaker so long as the specialist in Congress is primarily defined by the committee system. Occasionally senators are considered specialists because of their previous careers and without regard for their committee assignments. (Indeed, some such senators often seek to avoid the committee of their specialization.) In

24. "New Potential for Dividing Democrats," *Washington Post*, May 8, 1983; for the transcript of Dodd's speech, see *New York Times*, April 28, 1983.

25. Bernard Weinraub, "Mrs. Kirkpatrick Critical of Dodd," *New York Times*, May 1, 1983. Also see Rowland Evans and Robert Novak, "Those Other Democrats," *Washington Post*, May 6, 1983; and R. Emmett Tyrrell, Jr., "Dodd's Masterpiece," *Washington Post*, May 9, 1983.

26. Elisabeth Bumiller, "Christopher Dodd, His Father's Son," *Washington Post*, July 13, 1983.

most cases, however, the press continues to assign to a committee's members the right to be the experts in that field. The generalist in Congress, on the other hand, can make news by running for president, getting in trouble, or, to a much more modest degree than many have claimed, being a character.

IV

Being Newsworthy

ALTHOUGH MOST senators' media coverage is virtually predetermined by their place in the hierarchy of the Senate, their committee membership, and their association with particular issues, there are other determinants that are the subject of this chapter.

Each time a reporter described a senator, as Helen Dewar did the senior senator from Louisiana ("Russell B. Long, a powerful, colorful and wily lawmaker . . . "[1]), I put the clipping in a three-ring binder. Reporters often give us clues as to why they pay attention to certain senators by the words they put before or after the legislator's name. My collection of descriptive words may not explain how much news senators make, but it does suggest the characteristics that reporters find notable.

The distribution of Senate personality types—at least as depicted by the media's adjectives—resembles a bell-shaped curve. At one end of the curve is a small group of senators who might be thought of as the *originals*. From the reporters' perspective, they are obviously the most fun to write about:

1. "Russell Long Retiring From Senate in '86," *Washington Post*, February 26, 1985. According to Rochelle Jones and Peter Woll, *The Private World of Congress* (Free Press, 1979), p. 40, "Long worked hard to have the adjective 'wily' routinely affixed to his name."

Sen. Daniel Patrick Moynihan (D-New York), no stranger to melo-
drama . . . often has displayed a flair for drama in public life . . . the
thinking man's hawk . . . a politician known for his love of abstrac-
tions and theories . . . [2]

Senator Barry Goldwater of Arizona was here to speak his mind,
in his inimitable, unvarnished style . . . seems to take a perverse
delight in being provocative and unpredictable, usually in pungent
language . . . [3]

Besides Moynihan and Goldwater, this category would also include Bob Dole, Jesse Helms, Ernest Hollings, Edward Kennedy,
Russell Long, William Proxmire, and Alan Simpson. (Having a
stormy personal life is not what puts a Kennedy or a Long in this
group. John Warner and Donald Riegle, who also have had unusual marital relations, do not qualify as originals.)

Originals can get as much press coverage as they want on
subjects of general interest. A former Reuters editor says she
sprinkled quotations from Ted Kennedy in stories because he was
the one senator she could be sure that her overseas readers would
recognize. Lance Morgan, Senator Moynihan's press secretary,
notes that part of his job is declining requests for his boss to
appear on television programs that other senators covet.

Courting the press, however, is not a factor in becoming an
original. Helms does not hide his feelings about the news media or
its representatives. As he told a reporter for the *Raleigh News &
Observer*, "Your newspaper is a suck-egg mule."[4] Michael Cozza,

2. P. H. Terzian, "Congress Roils Foreign-Policy Waters," *Los Angeles Times*, April
19, 1984; John Machecek, "Angry Moynihan Quits Leadership Role on Panel," *USA
Today*, April 16, 1984; Michael Kramer, "Standing Pat," *New York Magazine*, August
20, 1984; and Lisa Wolfe, "Moynihan, as a Fellow at Columbia, Revels in a Return
to Campus Life," *New York Times*, February 26, 1985. Journalists seem to have a
fascination for certifiable intellectuals who succeed in elective politics, such as
Senators Henry Cabot Lodge, Sr. (R-Mass., 1893–1924), Albert J. Beveridge (R-Ind.,
1899–1911), and Paul Douglas (D-Ill., 1949–66). Moynihan, who continues to write
for learned publications of miniscule circulation, currently occupies the Senate's
intellectual-in-residence chair. See Stephen Hess, "Ideas and Politics: Unusual
Alliance," *Baltimore Sun*, January 28, 1980.

3. Martin Tolchin, "Goldwater, Ignoring Laxalt Plea, Speaks His Mind at G.O.P.
Parley," *New York Times*, August 23, 1984; and Bill Keller, "Rattling the Pentagon's
Coffee Cups," *New York Times*, December 17, 1984.

4. Fred Barnes, "Presswatch," *The American Spectator*, vol. 17 (July 1984), p. 24.

who covers Washington for a Charlotte, North Carolina, television station, wonders whether we are on or off the record, then says, "on the record, Helms is probably the most difficult person in the Senate; other reporters will agree." The *Washington Post*'s Dewar does agree, "Yet the irony is Helms is also one of the most accessible senators. It's not difficult to get him to come off the [Senate] floor to talk with you even if he won't say much." On the other hand, Alan Simpson obviously loves journalists. Nothing seems to give him as much pleasure as to argue with a reporter who disagrees with him. "Do you need them?" I ask. "I couldn't get an immigration bill through without Tony Day and Bob Erburu, Jack Rosenthal and Meg Greenfield," he replies. (His choice of names suggests that he has given more study to the news business than he chooses to admit.)[5] Martin Tolchin of the *New York Times* tells of going to Wyoming to do a story on a Simpson campaign: "In Casper, Simpson said, 'there's one editor who really hates what I stand for, always attacks me. I want you to meet him.' He then took me and the editor to dinner." Tolchin adds, "Simpson is the only person in the Senate with the ego strength to take me to dinner to meet his worst critic." The Wyoming senator also has developed an interesting technique for staying out of newspapers and off TV when he wants to: he simply expresses an opinion in such barnyard language as to ensure that no reporter will quote him. "I think the Senate is beginning to look like a bunch of jackasses" (a comment by Barry Goldwater) is about as gamy as an editor will permit in a "family" news outlet.[6]

A sure sign that a senator is considered an original by the press is the variety of topics on which he is asked to comment. (The exception is Proxmire, whose single theme is the "Golden Fleece" of government waste.) As already noted, the usual pattern is for

5. Anthony Day is the editorial page editor of the *Los Angeles Times*; Robert F. Erburu is president and chief executive officer of Times Mirror, which publishes the *Los Angeles Times* and other newspapers; Jack Rosenthal is deputy editorial page editor of the *New York Times*; and Meg Greenfield is editorial page editor of the *Washington Post*.

6. Martin Tolchin, "Requiem for the Filibuster," *New York Times*, October 4, 1984. Simpson has been quoted as saying that his bald head is "the solar panel for a sex machine" in E. Michael Myers (UPI), "Senate Wits Cushion Their Hits," *Los Angeles Times*, November 3, 1985.

reporters to seek out senators because of their expertise: of the nineteen times that Christopher Dodd was seen on the networks' evening news programs in 1983, sixteen appearances related to U.S. policy in Central America; of Sam Nunn's nine appearances, eight were about U.S. military posture. But an original such as Moynihan could be seen commenting on eleven different topics, including social security, the proposal to make Martin Luther King's birthday a national holiday, the invasion of Grenada, a boycott of the St. Patrick's Day parade, unemployment, U.S.-Soviet relations, the death of Senator Henry Jackson, and various aspects of the race for the Democratic presidential nomination. The implication was that a comment by Moynihan, regardless of the subject, would help the story.

Few originals seem to be left in the Senate, however. Walter Mears, a former chief Senate correspondent for the Associated Press, remembers that in the 1960s "a quote from Dirksen or Humphrey could carry a story." When Dirksen addressed the Senate on January 11, 1960, for example, it was to introduce legislation to make the marigold the "national floral emblem" of the United States. "So hardy, so lovely, so easy to grow, so diffused, so long-blooming," declared the Senator from Illinois, "I have taken real delight in producing a few prize marigolds."[7] This sort of orating is not heard anymore, according to Dennis Beal, a long-tenured press secretary now with the Budget Committee. Writing in 1963, Allen Drury of *Advise and Consent* fame recalled the "delightful characters" of the 1943 Senate, when he was a reporter for United Press, and bemoaned the present lot: "the suits are Brooks Brothers, the air is junior-executive."[8] It was a complaint heard from another generation of oldtimers in 1983, recalling the delightful characters of 1963. It may be, of course, that there never were many originals, just our memories playing tricks. (Congressional correspondents also seem less colorful characters than they used to be, say veterans of the Washington press corps like Don Shannon of the *Los Angeles Times*. He recalled a reporter named Blair Moody who in 1951 went from the *Detroit News* to an appoint-

7. *Congressional Record* (January 11, 1960), pp. 200–01.
8. A *Senate Journal*, 1943–1945 (McGraw-Hill, 1963; rprt. New York: De Capo Press, 1972), p. 2.

ment as a U.S. senator and on whom the reporters dropped spit-balls whenever he sat in the presiding officer's chair directly below the press gallery.)[9]

Although political scientists and others claim that television is producing a new style of senator—the individualistic attention-grabber—my collection of press descriptions suggests that this view needs to be modified. Indeed, whether the suit is Brooks Brothers or not, the largest group of senators could be the *low-keys*:

> Senator Richard G. Lugar (R-Indiana) is known as a low-key, diligent, intelligent man . . . a calm and steady politician who does not in-dulge in temper tantrums or sarcasm . . . smart and hard-working, but he is anything but flashy . . . [10]

> Senator Nancy Landon Kassebaum (R-Kansas) is a low-key, mild-mannered politician . . . more prone to study and work behind the scenes for compromise than grab headlines . . . no publicity hound.[11]

> Senator Bill Bradley (D-New Jersey) whom friends describe as quiet and private by nature. . . . Often he speaks in a quiet mono-tone. . . . [12]

> Senator Lawton Chiles (D-Florida), an unpretentious lawmaker . . . a plain-spoken person who doesn't often grab headlines . . . a low-keyed southerner . . . [13]

> Senator Howard Baker (R-Tennessee) . . . easygoing, conciliatory personality . . . low-key approach . . . Those of us who have watched

9. See Richard L. Riedel, "A View from the President's Room," in Robert O. Blanchard, ed., *Congress and the News Media* (Hastings House, 1974), p. 277.

10. Margaret Shapiro, "Lugar Usually Backs Reagan Foreign Policy," *Washington Post*, November 29, 1984; Marianne Means, "Lugar Targeted for GOP Leader," King Features Syndicate, May 17, 1984; and Christopher Madison, "Lugar's Prime Task on Foreign Relations Is to Try to Restore the Panel's Luster," *National Journal*, vol. 16, (December 8, 1984), p. 2343.

11. Leslie Phillips, "Kassebaum Shuns GOP 'Ladies' Night,' " *USA Today*, August 23, 1984; and *Congressional Quarterly Weekly Report*, vol. 42 (February 25, 1984), p. 373. Also see Dennis Farney, "Kassebaum Passes Political Muster," *Wall Street Journal*, September 26, 1984.

12. Michael Winerip, "Bradley is Running Poised Campaign," *New York Times*, October 31, 1984.

13. Desda Moss, "Senator Filibusters for Fiscal Restraint," *USA Today*, August 8, 1984; and Helen Dewar, "Chiles to Seek Minority Leader Post," *Washington Post*, December 7, 1984.

Howard Baker from the press gallery for the past four years might credit his remarkable success to a single quality: patience.[14]

According to other press accounts, William Cohen (R-Maine), Charles Grassley (R-Iowa), and Walter Huddleston (D-Kentucky) are *easy-going*;[15] William Armstrong (R-Colorado), George Mitchell (D-Maine), and Thad Cochran (R-Mississippi) are *soft-spoken*;[16] Quentin Burdick (D-North Dakota) and Carl Levin (D-Michigan) are *self-effacing*;[17] Charles Mathias (R-Maryland) and Paul Laxalt (R-Nevada) have *quiet charm*.[18] Others are *mild-mannered* and *even-tempered*.[19] In all, I counted thirty-four senators in this category, of whom eight were in the top third of the national media ranking, thirteen in the middle, and thirteen in the bottom third.[20]

Even some senators who cannot be classified as low-key are now said by the press to have *mellowed*, notably Strom Thurmond and Bob Dole, as in "Today the hatchet man image has faded. According to friends, Dole mellowed after marrying Elizabeth Hanford. . . ."[21]

Perhaps the temperature of the Senate reflects to some extent the style of the majority leader. Most of these low-key readings were recorded during the tenure of Howard Baker, a patient man

14. Dennis Farney, "Baker is Ready for 'Civilian' Life," *Wall Street Journal*, August 8, 1984; and James J. Kilpatrick, "The Senate's Man of Patience," *Washington Post*, November 18, 1984.

15. *Congressional Quarterly Weekly Report*, vol. 42 (February 25, 1984), pp. 374, 376; and Alan Ehrenhalt, ed., *Politics in America* (CQ Press, 1984), p. 527.

16. *Politics in America*, pp. 226, 639; and *Congressional Quarterly Weekly Report*, vol. 42 (February 25, 1984), p. 387.

17. *Politics in America*, p. 1150; and Michael Barone and Grant Ujifusa, *The Almanac of American Politics 1984* (National Journal, 1983), p. 571.

18. David S. Broder, "Mathias and Laxalt," *Washington Post*, October 2, 1985.

19. *Politics in America*, pp. 275, 385.

20. Those not previously listed are James Abdnor (R-S.Dak.), John Chafee (R-R.I.), Dennis DeConcini (D-Ariz.), David Durenburger (R-Minn.), Daniel Evans (R-Wash.), J. James Exon (D-Nebr.), Wendell Ford (D-Ky.), John Glenn (D-Ohio), J. Bennett Johnston (D-La.), Patrick Leahy (D-Vt.), James McClure (R-Idaho), Spark Matsunaga (D-Hawaii), Mack Mattingly (R-Ga.), Frank Murkowski (R-Alaska), Sam Nunn (D-Ga.), William Roth (R-Del.), Paul Sarbanes (D-Md.), Robert Stafford (R-Vt.), and John Stennis (D-Miss.).

21. Margaret Shapiro, "Dole Known for Wit, Legislative Prowess," *Washington Post*, November 29, 1984; and Martin Tolchin, "New Leader of the Senate," *New York Times*, November 29, 1984. For Strom Thurmond as "a mellowed elder statesman," see *Congressional Quarterly Weekly Report*, vol. 42 (February 25, 1984), p. 413.

according to James J. Kilpatrick. As for his successor, Bob Dole says of himself, "I'm sort of impatient."[22]

The group at the other end of the curve, the *volatiles*, includes Alfonse D'Amato (*quick temper . . . temperamental*), Jeremiah Denton (*a sailor's tongue*), Paula Hawkins (*feisty . . . flamboyant, flip style . . . a scrappy, catch-as-catch-can sort of woman*), John Heinz (*a stubborn man with a tendency to become quarrelsome*), Roger Jepsen (*brusque*), Howard Metzenbaum (*a natural irritant*), Ted Stevens (*quick temper and stubborn nature*), Steve Symms (*eccentric*), Lowell Weicker (*volatile and voluble*), and Edward Zorinsky (*cranky*).[23]

The originals and the volatiles have certain similarities. They seem colorful compared with their colleagues in the middle, tending to be volubly opinionated and often quick to call attention to themselves. What, then, distinguishes them from each other? Not ideology or party. There are liberals and conservatives, Republicans and Democrats, in both categories. The originals, however, are more likely to have a sense of humor. When Senators Dole and Simpson were elected majority leader and whip, respectively, in late November 1984, the *Washington Post* editorialized, "they are, if not Capitol Hill's two funniest men, at least among the top five. (We mean intentionally funny, as distinct from the other kind, which abounds up there.)"[24] The originals are also the more interesting public speakers. Reporters earn their livelihood with words, and they have a fondness for those who use language in unusual

22. Andy Plattner, "Dole on the Job: Keeping the Senate Running," *Congressional Quarterly Weekly Report*, vol. 43 (June 29, 1985), p. 1269.

23. J. D. Solomon, "Al D'Amato Picks Up Speed," *New Rochelle* (N.Y.) *Standard-Star*, August 12, 1984; Jeffrey H. Birnbaum, "Lobbyists Are Looking for a Break," *Wall Street Journal*, June 15, 1984; Ehrenhalt, *Politics in America*, p. 12; Sheila Caudle, "Hawkins Knows Fear of Abuse," *USA Today*, April 27, 1984; Dinesh D'Souza, "Paths to Victory," *Policy Review* (Summer 1984), p. 48; Ehrenhalt, *Politics in America*, p. 1276; John Hyde, "Roger on the Run," *New Republic* (October 1, 1984), p. 20; Martin Tolchin, "Senate's Self-Appointed Watchdog," *New York Times*, March 22, 1984; *Congressional Quarterly Weekly Report*, vol. 42 (February 25, 1984), p. 348; Ehrenhalt, *Politics in America*, p. 397; Mary McGrory, "Garrulous Lowell Weicker Speaks Volumes by Merely Walking," *Washington Post*, August 9, 1984; and Ehrenhalt, *Politics in America*, p. 900.

24. "The Dole and Simpson Show," *Washington Post*, November 29, 1984; also see "The Wit and Wisdom of Dole and Simpson," *Los Angeles Times*, November 3, 1985; and David Shribman, "Washington Humor: Bob and Al Succeed Ev and Charlie Show," *Wall Street Journal*, January 21, 1986.

ways. But most important, the originals tend to be powerful and
the volatiles tend not to be, suggesting again that the distinctions
reporters make among senators are largely in the eyes of the
beholders, and, although they may affect the quality of a legislator's coverage, the quantity is overwhelmingly a product of position. Had Ted Stevens been elected majority leader instead of Bob
Dole—he lost on a 28-25 vote—the irascible Alaska senator instantly would have been transformed from a volatile to an original, just as after Richard Lugar became chairman of the Foreign
Relations Committee in 1985 a reporter discovered an occasional
"glimmer of humor" that apparently he had not noticed before.[25]

Reporters also like their senators to be a little unpredictable (it
is more interesting) but not too much (it is flaky).[26] As a case in
point, Charles Grassley has become relatively well covered by the
press. By 1983 the Iowa Republican had a higher national media
rating than thirteen of his colleagues in the Class of 1980 and was
surpassed in attention by only four. Grassley's attractiveness to
the press is that he has not always acted as expected. His advance
billing was as a lock-step member of the New Right, so when he
started to call attention to waste in the military and even proposed a freeze on military spending, he was sufficiently out of
character to be newsworthy. The Des Moines Register's headline on a
flattering profile of Grassley's first three years in office was "HE'D
RATHER BE RIGHT THAN 'RIGHT.' "[27]

Personality is a modest determinant of what news comes from
the Senate. Recall that when I quantified the adjectives used in the
Los Angeles Times and USA Today for a six-month period (see table
2-3), personal characteristics ranked third (17 percent), behind
expertise on issues (19 percent) and senators' leadership and
committee positions (38 percent). But when I asked all the TV
network correspondents in the Senate to tell me which senators

---

25. Robert S. Greenberger, "Sen. Lugar Is Gaining New Prestige for Panel on
Foreign Relations," Wall Street Journal, November 1, 1985.

26. It may be that there are times when senators like to be unpredictable
because they know that reporters like unpredictability. Fred Barnes speculated
that Ted Kennedy voted for the Gramm-Rudman proposal on budget deficit reduction in 1985 as "an attempt at being unpredictable." See "Kennedy The Front-
Runner," New Republic (November 25, 1985), p. 18.

27. John Hyde, Des Moines Register, January 29, 1984.

they most liked to interview, many of the names mentioned were originals, some were low-keys, and the fewest were volatiles, even though several in the latter category made a good deal of news.

Take Nancy Kassebaum and Paula Hawkins as examples. Scarcity being a factor in newsworthiness, one might think that the only two women senators would get a lot of media attention. They do not. But Kassebaum gets more than Hawkins, two-and-a-half times as much according to the 1983 national media ranking. Attention from inner-ring national news organizations has little to do with a senator's press operation, as noted earlier. Still, Hawkins's effort to be noticed might show up in the tabulations of secondary media appearances in table B-11. Yet again Kassebaum's rating is slightly higher, and she also gets on programs of greater prominence, such as "The Today Show" and "Good Morning America." Part of the disparity has to do with the issues on which the senators have chosen to concentrate: Kassebaum's— foreign policy and the budget—are considered more "serious" by the national media; Hawkins's—drug use and child abuse—are more marginal by the standards of what stories make the networks' evening news.

More important, the greater attention paid Kassebaum represents a trend in national news coverage: the reaction to hype on the part of reporters is now such that, all other factors being held constant, the individualistic attention-grabbing senator is at a disadvantage in appearing on network evening news and the Sunday interview programs or being mentioned in the newsmagazines and serious newspapers.[28] When talking about Kassebaum, the *Washington Post*'s Helen Dewar approvingly notes that the senator "readily admits she's not much of a [public] speaker."

Journalists increasingly do not want to think that they are being sold a story, especially on Capitol Hill, which, in the words of the *Wall Street Journal*'s David Rogers, is "a big rock candy mountain for reporters." This is another reason why the data in this study refuse to support the widely held thesis that the future of politics on the

28. For Hawkins's assertive media strategy, see Ellen Hume, " 'Narco-Terrorism,' Other Dramatic Media Topics Make Congress's Oversight Hearings Political Art," *Wall Street Journal*, November 1, 1985; and Bill Peterson, "Hawkins Puts Campaign on the Nightly 'Feed,' " *Washington Post*, November 9, 1985.

national level belongs to the blow-dried politicians. Note the contrasting models suggested by two senators' press relations in the following excerpts, as well as the writers' clear indication of approval or disapproval:

> One model for a successful Senate debut was set by Sen. Bill Bradley (D-New Jersey). . . . Eager to demonstrate that he wasn't out to win easy headlines, Mr. Bradley turned down interview requests from reporters representing national newspapers. He wouldn't talk to sportswriters. . . . He sought to build a reputation for thoroughness. The result was a reputation among national political reporters for being cerebral, even a bit dull, and a reputation among his colleagues for—praise of praise in the Senate—being thoughtful.[29]

> Arlen Specter, Republican of Pennsylvania, is the model of how to build a Senate career through manipulation of the media. . . . [He] brings new and impressive audacity to senatorial hype. . . . Specter continues to push hard for any media opportunity. . . . Friends and associates often privately lament that Specter does not apply his intelligence more constructively.[30]

Choosing to quote one senator rather than another also partly reflects the personal preferences of reporters. Julia Malone of the *Christian Science Monitor* explains that when writing a "reaction" story—"What is your reaction to the bombing of the Marine barracks in Lebanon?"—after seeking out the leaders and the experts ("the mandatory types"), her quotations will be based on whom she can reach, whom she has established relations with (meaning who, based on past experience, will promptly return calls), who puts out statements, and who is known to have interesting (often meaning unpredictable) things to say.

Just as reporters seem to be attracted almost magnetically to certain types, other types can be counted on to repel them. Based on my press gallery conversations, I found that the repellent legislators fall into two unequal categories. Those in the lesser group are usually described as boy scouts; there is a cooky-cutter sameness to their values and sometimes even to their appearance. The

29. David Shribman, "Paul Simon of Illinois Makes a Mark in Senate . . ." *Wall Street Journal*, August 1, 1985.

30. Murray Waas, "Media Specter," *New Republic* (September 30, 1985), pp. 13–15.

major criticism, however, is reserved for senators who are considered pompous. Pomposity is the deadliest sin. Russ Ward of NBC radio mentions two young senators who, he says, are honest, intelligent, and hardworking, but he does not like to be around them—*they are pompous*. And because they are not powerful (hence not necessary to him), he chooses other senators when he needs a quotation for filler. Dorothy Collin of the *Chicago Tribune* even has a theory about pomposity in the Senate. She thinks that young senators start off pompous, mellow in their middle years, and then return to a pompous old age.

Senate reporters make the same choices in picking which characteristics to write about as do reporters who cover people in other lines of work. Height gets mentioned if the subject is tall or short (Simpson or Baker), weight if lean or pudgy (Cranston or Boren). An unusual previous occupation (astronaut or professional basketball player) may also be noted. Deviations from the norm are what attract attention.

Two characteristics among senators are handled differently, however. The U.S. Senate is composed of people who are mostly handsome. One young senator bears a resemblance to Robert Redford. Looking down on roll calls from the press gallery, I have counted at least twenty senators who could pose for Arrow shirt ads. Yet in my year of underlining adjectives, I found only two senators, Roger Jepsen and Barry Goldwater, described by reporters as *handsome*. A senator apparently cannot be handsome until his hair is gray, although he is more often called "silver-haired" (Lautenberg, Hollings) or "white-haired."[31] Only then does a senator look senatorial. "Although few lawmakers look more senatorial than Jepsen, the 'quality' of the handsome, white-haired senator is generally seen as his most vulnerable point," wrote Julia Malone of the *Christian Science Monitor* in January 1984.[32] This is not a new phenomenon, of course. Allen Drury wrote in his diary in December 1943, "Guy Gillette of Iowa and Hugh Butler of Nebraska. vie

31. Jane Perlez, "Working Profile: Frank R. Lautenberg," *New York Times*, July 19, 1984; and Robert Mackay (UPI), "Hollings' Eye on Senate Leadership?" Columbia (S.C.) *State*, March 7, 1984.

32. "Iowa GOP Senator was Slipping—Until his Opponent Emerged," *Christian Science Monitor*, January 19, 1984.

for the title of Most Senatorial. Both are model solons, white-haired, dignified. . . ."[33]

Money is the other characteristic treated in a special way. The Senate included thirty millionaires in 1984, according to one report,[34] but only a few are regularly identified as wealthy. Those whose riches are mentioned are either associated with a brand name—"heir to the Ralston-Purina fortune"—or are "self-made millionaires."[35] The ideologies of the Senate's millionaires also interest reporters. When I asked Howard Metzenbaum's press secretary, Roy Meyers, what adjective the senator likes to see before his name, Meyers replied, "I can tell you what he hates: 'liberal millionaire.' " ("We love oxymorons," replies a reporter.) Only once in my clippings is a senator (John Warner) described as a "conservative millionaire."[36]

The personal characteristics that senators bring to Washington, then, do have some effect on the way they are received by the congressional press corps. But what can be said of the senators' political characteristics—where they fit along the ideological spectrum—and whether these too affect coverage?

A senator's ideology, as we have seen in one tabulation, accounts for 9 percent of the adjectives attached to his name in two major newspapers.[37] It is not Jesse Helms's personality that intrigues reporters, who are constantly searching for new terms to describe his conservatism (*fiery, unflagging*, as well as the more traditional *ultra-* and *arch-*).[38] But will a senator be more noticed as a liberal or a conservative, Republican or Democrat?

In an earlier study I examined how the three television net-

33. A *Senate Journal*, p. 11.

34. Pat Ordovensky and Richard Benedetto, "High Price, High Rewards of Public Life," USA *Today*, May 21, 1984.

35. Helen Dewar, " 'Senator of Conscience' Guides Commerce Panel," *Washington Post*, December 31, 1984 (about John Danforth); and Martin Tolchin, "Working Profile: Howard M. Metzenbaum," *New York Times*, March 22, 1984.

36. Marianne Means, "Washington Sideshow," King Features Syndicate, February 15, 1984.

37. See p. 21.

38. See, for example, Marta McCave, "D'Aubuisson and Helms: Bedfellows on the Ultra-Right," USA *Today*, June 27, 1984.

works' evening news programs and twenty-two newspapers covered Congress during seven days in April 1978. The results for the Senate were that television coverage of Republicans trailed that of Democrats by 17 percent; the overall figures showed that the Democrats received 10 percent more coverage than the Republicans. Looking at what was then a Democratic-controlled Senate, I wrote,

> Some will contend that this is evidence of a Democratic leaning in the Washington press corps. Others could argue that 10 percent represents a press bonus to the majority party. Whenever a committee chairman is quoted, for example, that person has to be a Democrat. "Reporters don't care what the Republicans say simply because they're not in control," says a young Washington reporter. With Republicans taking control in 1981, the proposition should be tested.[39]

When Congress convened in 1981 there were forty-seven Democrats and fifty-three Republicans in the Senate. (In both 1978 and 1981 Harry F. Byrd, Jr., elected as an independent, was counted with the Democrats because he received his committee assignments through the Democratic caucus.) The majority Republicans got 57 percent of the mentions on the network evening news program during 1981–82, a 4 percent bonus.

In computing the figures for 1983, I excluded all items that were about senators solely because they were considered potential presidential candidates, not a factor that would have inflated the 1978 data.

As table 4-1 suggests, there is a majority bonus, but it is not as great for Republicans as for Democrats. (One journalist contends that the Washington press corps reported on a Democratic Senate for so long that these data mainly reflect reporters' tardiness in adjusting to the reality of Republican senators as being the chief sources of news. In short, he says, it takes time to remember that Russell Long is no longer "Mr. Chairman" on the Finance Committee.)

The question of to what degree the press factors a senator's ideology into newsworthiness is more complicated. There are only two political parties represented in Congress, but how many po-

39. Stephen Hess, *The Washington Reporters* (Brookings, 1981), p. 103.

Table 4-1. *Media Coverage of Senators by Party, 1978 and 1983*
Percent

Item	Senate composition	Media coverage	Bonus
1978			
Democrats	59	69	+10
Republicans	41	31	
1983			
Republicans	54	59	+ 5
Democrats	46	41	

litical ideologies are there? In the 1984 clippings, for example, Alan Cranston is described as an *ultraliberal* in one article and merely a *liberal* in another, Lowell Weicker is a *liberal Republican* and a *moderate*, Lawton Chiles is both a *moderate conservative* and a *conservative*. Liberal or conservative on what? Alan Baron points out, "In 1983, on economics, Senator Percy voted 15% liberal; Senator Dixon, 85%. But on social and foreign issues, Senator Dixon was to the right of Senator Percy."[40] Baron, therefore, devised three separate scales to measure relative liberalism or conservatism on economic issues, social issues, and foreign policy issues. The scales have been used by *National Journal* since 1981.[41]

Table 4-2 adapts Baron's three scales to the 1983 media ranking (we had almost identical results using the Foote-Weber listing of network television mentions for 1981–82). The table focuses only on the top third of the senators, who represent 80 percent of the entire Senate's media score. Senators are listed in rank order according to their overall media scores (see table 2-2).

On each scale, senators in the top third among liberals are listed in italics, and those in the top third among conservatives are

40. "For Truth in Political Labeling," *Wall Street Journal*, May 7, 1984.

41. See Richard E. Cohen, "Rating Congress—A Guide to Separating the Liberals from the Conservatives," *National Journal*, vol. 14 (May 8, 1982), pp. 800–10; William Schneider, "Party Unity on Tax, Spending Issues—Less in House, More in Senate in 1982," *National Journal*, vol. 15 (May 7, 1983), pp. 936–52; and William Schneider, "Democrats, Republicans Move Further Apart on Most Issues in 1983 Session," *National Journal*, vol. 16 (May 12, 1984), pp. 904–20.

Table 4-2. *Senator Ideology and Media Coverage, 1983*

Economic issues	Foreign policy issues	Social issues
21L Glenn (D-Ohio)	Glenn	13L Glenn
19L Cranston (D-Calif.)	5L Cranston	Cranston
20C BAKER (R-Tenn.)	32C BAKER	Baker
28C DOLE (R-Kans.)	4C DOLE	16C DOLE
20L Hart (D-Colo.)	15L Hart	12L Hart
32L Hollings (D-S.C.)	33L Hollings	Hollings
2L Kennedy (D-Mass.)	10L Kennedy	1L Kennedy
6C HELMS (R-N.C.)	5C HELMS	7C HELMS
Domenici (R-N.Mex.)	Domenici	Domenici
18L Moynihan (D-N.Y.)	18L Moynihan	14L Moynihan
3L Jackson (D-Wash.)	Jackson	Jackson
19C TOWER (R-Tex.)	23C TOWER	30C TOWER
Mathias (R-Md.)	30L Mathias	27L Mathias
33C PERCY (R-Ill.)	Percy	18L Percy
15L Dodd (D-Conn.)	6L Dodd	11L Dodd
16C LAXALT (R-Nev.)	19C LAXALT	16C LAXALT
6L Byrd (D-W.Va.)	Byrd	Byrd
6C HATCH (R-Utah)	24C HATCH	2C HATCH
14L Tsongas (D-Mass.)	1L Tsongas	1L Tsongas
5C GOLDWATER (R-Ariz.)	1C GOLDWATER	Goldwater
31C KASTEN (R-Wis.)	2C KASTEN	13C KASTEN
Nunn (D-Ga.)	Nunn	Nunn
Packwood (R-Oreg.)	Packwood	30L Packwood
4L Metzenbaum (D-Ohio)	23L Metzenbaum	1L Metzenbaum
Hatfield (R-Oreg.)	2L Hatfield	24L Hatfield
Chiles (D-Fla.)	Chiles	31L Chiles
22L Bumpers (D-Ark.)	31L Bumpers	25L Bumpers
4L Levin (D-Mich.)	4L Levin	1L Levin
Stevens (R-Alaska)	32C STEVENS	Stevens
Weicker (R-Conn.)	17L Weicker	27L Weicker
17C ARMSTRONG (R-Colo.)	6C ARMSTRONG	20C ARMSTRONG
D'Amato (R-N.Y.)	3C D'AMATO	23C D'AMATO
4L Biden (D-Del.)	20L Biden	Biden

capitalized. The way to read the table from left to right: John
Glenn, who had the highest media score for 1983, was the twenty-
first most liberal senator on economic issues, did not rank in the
top thirty-three liberal or conservative senators on foreign policy
issues, and was the thirteenth most liberal senator on social issues. Howard Baker, whose media score ranked him third in 1983,
had the twentieth most conservative voting record on economics,
the thirty-second most conservative voting record on foreign policy, and was not among the top third of the Senate, either as a
conservative or a liberal, on social issues. (Some senators have the
same voting record; thus Howard Metzenbaum, Carl Levin, and
Joseph Biden are all listed as the fourth most liberal senator on
economic issues.)

  The top third of the Senate, the media's elite, included fourteen
liberals and ten conservatives on economic issues and fourteen
liberals and eleven conservatives on foreign policy. The widest
division came on social issues: fifteen liberals and eight conservatives. Most of the differences can be accounted for by Republican
Senators Charles Mathias, Mark Hatfield, and Lowell Weicker voting as liberals on social and foreign policy issues and being joined
by two other Republicans, Charles Percy and Bob Packwood, on
social issues. Hatfield was elected in 1966; Packwood, Mathias and
Percy in 1968; Weicker in 1970. There is a careful correlation
between seniority and press attention, and it happens that the
more liberal Republicans in the Senate are among the GOP's more
senior senators.

  Using the "Network Roundup" data for July 1982, the Senate
Republican Conference reached a similar conclusion: the senators
who appear on television public affairs programs rate more liberal
on Baron's social issues scale than on either of the scales measur-
ing their votes on economics or foreign policy issues. This is true
for both Republicans and Democrats, although the differences are
far greater for Republicans.[42]

  42. The Senate Republican Conference concluded that for July 1982, "the composite average of Republican [senators'] appearances on nationally distributed
television was 7.68 economic, 11.0 foreign/defense, 17.25 social; the composite
average of Democratic appearance . . . 80.57 economic, 80.57 foreign/defense,
85.41 social [based on a scale of 0 = conservative to 100 = liberal]." James J.

It cannot be assumed that every time senators are quoted in the press they are saying something "liberal" or "conservative." This is not a content analysis. These data simply indicate that from 1981 through 1983 liberal senators, especially as measured by their votes on social issues, got more attention from the national news media than did conservative senators. The data, however, could add fuel to the controversy over whether or not there is a liberal tilt to the news.[43] Most studies indicate that reporters are more liberal than the rest of the nation.[44] A *Los Angeles Times* poll, for example, found that only 26 percent of the newspaper journalists in its sample voted for President Reagan in 1984.[45] Whether this rubs off on what appears in the press is another matter.[46] The Clancey-Robinson survey of the 1984 presidential campaign concluded that "74 percent of the total time on network evening news devoted to national candidates had no clear spin, negative or positive," but when there was a slant, it was positive for the Mondale-Ferraro ticket and negative for candidates Reagan and

---

Kilpatrick proposed that a senator's conservative/liberal score should be computed by combining two conservative organizations' rating (Chamber of Commerce and Americans for Constitutional Action), combining two liberal organizations' rating (AFL-CIO and Americans for Democratic Action), and then subtracting one from the other. In his column, "Arches and Ultras" (*Washington Post*, June 28, 1984), Kilpatrick listed the twenty most conservative senators and the twenty most liberal. Applying the data from our 1983 national media ranking to Kilpatrick's list shows a wide margin in favor of the liberals—62 percent to 38 percent.

43. See Nick Thimmesch, ed., *A Liberal Media Elite?* (American Enterprise Institute, 1985), which includes the "answers" of Ben Bradlee, Rupert Murdoch, Robert Lichter, and Michael Massing.

44. In 1936, Leo Rosten found the Washington press corps even more overwhelmingly in favor of Franklin Roosevelt than the electorate; after Richard Nixon's landslide victory of 1972, a study of the Washington press corps found that a majority voted Democratic. See Leo C. Rosten, *The Washington Correspondents* (Harcourt, Brace, 1937; rprt. Arno Press, 1974), pp. 59–60; and Lewis W. Wolfson, study director, *The Press Covers Government: The Nixon Years from 1969 to Watergate* (American University and the National Press Club, 1973), p. 6. Also see S. Robert Lichter and Stanley Rothman, "Media and Business Elites," *Public Opinion* (October/November 1981), esp. table 2, "Presidential Voting Record of Media Elite, 1964–1976."

45. David Shaw, "Public and Press—Two Viewpoints," *Los Angeles Times*, August 11, 1985; also see Shaw, "Media: High Ratings are Tempered," *Los Angeles Times*, August 12, 1985.

46. For a rebuttal of the "liberal media" contentions, see Albert R. Hunt, "Media Bias Is in Eye of the Beholder," *Wall Street Journal*, July 23, 1985.

Bush, although this was attributed to nonideological factors, such as incumbency. ("Reporters simply feel that they have a special mission to warn Americans about the advantages any incumbent has.")[47] From the year I spent in the Senate press gallery I came away with the feeling that senators' ideology had little to do with reporters' personal likes and dislikes. When I asked reporters to list the senators they most liked to interview, they frequently mentioned conservatives—Barry Goldwater, Bob Dole, Howard Baker, and Alan Simpson. The reporters also wanted to tell me their "least favorite." Jesse Helms was often mentioned ("testy"), but so too was Ted Kennedy whose reputation, according to Fred Barnes, is "as the nation's foremost reflexive liberal."[48]

Just as ideology and party affiliation affect press coverage of senators, so too can a senator's relationship with colleagues. It is a phenomenon of the Senate noted as long ago as 1960 that "the relations between two Senators from the same state are almost always strained."[49] Ross K. Baker writes of *feud, hostility, rivalry, bad blood*, and *personal vendetta*.[50] He also recounts some warm friendships, including what he calls "the mentor-protegé" relationship between senators of the same state, but, he rightly concludes, these are "fast disappearing."[51]

"A state of formal détente between New York's Senators, Daniel Patrick Moynihan and Alfonse M. D'Amato, has apparently done little to mask continuing tensions," the New York Times de-

47. Maura Clancey and Michael J. Robinson, "General Election Coverage: Part 1," Public Opinion (December/January 1985), pp. 50, 54.

48. Fred Barnes, "Kennedy the Front-Runner," New Republic (November 25, 1985), p. 16.

49. Donald R. Matthews, U.S. Senators & Their World (Vintage, 1960), p. 216.

50. Baker, who had been an aide to three senators before turning to academics, cites as his examples Walter George and Richard Russell (Georgia), Wayne Morse and Richard Neuberger (Oregon), J. William Fulbright and John McClellan (Arkansas), Birch Bayh and Vance Hartke (Indiana), Richard Schweicker and John Heinz (Pennsylvania), and Mark Hatfield and Bob Packwood (Oregon). Friend and Foe in the U.S. Senate (Free Press, 1980), pp. 17, 57, 71, 71. Also see Adrian C. Taylor, "The Flacks of the Hill," Washington Journalism Review, vol. 1 (June/July 1979), pp. 42–43.

51. Friend and Foe, pp. 20–22, 154–55. Among the friendships listed are Walter Mondale and Hubert Humphrey (Minnesota), Herman Talmadge and Sam Nunn (Georgia), and Russell Long and J. Bennett Johnston (Louisiana).

clared under the headline, IN WASHINGTON, NEW YORK'S SENATORS AT
ODDS, on May 21, 1984. "Sitting side by side at a rare joint appearance before the press several weeks ago, Mr. Moynihan, the cere-
bral Democrat, and Mr. D'Amato, the visceral Republican, heaped
praise on each other," wrote reporter Jane Perlez. "Behind the
scenes, though, bickering continues. . . . There is the question of
what Mr. Moynihan's staff sees as Mr. D'Amato's more aggressive
approach to publicity."

Perlez considered the competition for publicity as one of the
causes of strain between two senators from the same state, or, at
least, between the senators' staffs. Bill Hendrix, Jake Garn's press
secretary, recalls that at one time both Utah senators had press
secretaries who had been Salt Lake City television reporters, and
"our competition [in Washington] was almost like [that] between
rival stations." While such rivalries almost entirely involve the
making of local news, one assumes (but cannot prove) that some
of this competition also affects the effort made by senators and
their assistants to attract notice in the national media.

Despite the Moynihan-D'Amato example, most of the tensions
that reporters told me about were between senators of the same
party; the better relations were between senators of different parties. A Democratic senator from the Midwest said of his cooper-
ative relationship with the Republican senator from his state, "I'll
deny it if you quote me, but a state is better off having a senator
from each party. I'll spot a problem and work it up and he'll carry it
to the White House. Of course it would be different if both houses
and the presidency were Democratic."[52] Murray Flander, press
secretary to Democrat Alan Cranston, who gets on very well with
California's other senator, Republican Pete Wilson, says that a
state's two senators are on different election timetables and will
never run against each other, but senators of the same party are
competing for the same constituencies; thus, he concludes, it is
for psychological rather than electoral reasons that a state's sena-

TENSION

52. According to Kevin Phillips, Democratic Senator Sam Nunn of Georgia has
made a "crypto-endorsement" of Republican colleague Mack Mattingly in his 1986
campaign for reelection; see *The American Political Report*, vol. 4 (April 19, 1985), p. 8.

tors are more apt to feel themselves in opposition to each other if they are of the same party.[53]

The frequency with which one senator overshadows his colleague—what Joe Foote and David Weber call "intrastate visibility imbalance"—is such that, based on an analysis of the networks' evening news in 1981–82, the two researchers suggest that there is "an institutionalized dominant-submissive role structure" in the Senate. They found that one senator received more than twice as much attention as the other in three-quarters of the states.[54]

Their data suggest to me that differences can be best explained by the large number of state delegations in which one member is part of the Senate's leadership (defined as including chairmen and ranking minority members of the committees) and the other is not in this select circle. Thus in 1983 there were significant disparities in the national news coverage of Howard Baker and James Sasser (Tennessee), Ted Stevens and Frank Murkowski (Alaska), Bob Dole and Nancy Kassebaum (Kansas), and Pete Domenici and Jeff Bingaman (New Mexico). The competition between a state's senators is most apt to affect how they approach the media when they are evenly matched, either both leaders—William Roth and Joseph Biden (Delaware), Mark Hatfield and Bob Packwood (Oregon), Strom Thurmond and Fritz Hollings (South Carolina)—or both nonleaders. According to Steve Forrester, a columnist for newspapers in the state of Washington, this is the way it works:

> Just last week, [Senator Slade] Gorton [R-Washington] appeared at the rostrum of the Senate Energy Committee, of which he is not a member. [Senator Daniel] Evans [R-Washington] was chairing the meeting, which concerned the federal debt of the Bonneville Power Administration. In the old days, Gorton's action would have been unthinkable, because committee jurisdiction meant something and senators did not simply show up at committee meetings where they

53. Of the 101 people who served in the Senate in 1983–84, only 4—Ohio Democrats Glenn and Metzenbaum and Pennsylvania Republicans Heinz and Specter—had ever opposed each other in an election, and the Glenn-Metzenbaum rivalry is legendary.

54. "Network Evening News Visibility of Congressmen and Senators," paper submitted to the 1984 annual Association for Education in Journalism and Mass Communication Convention, p. 4 and table 3.

did not belong. . . . Furthermore, Gorton's appearance detracted from the special fact that it was the first committee session chaired by Evans. Gorton departed not long after the television cameras had recorded his remarks.

Forrester concluded, "the relationship between two senators from any state is always precarious. It is especially so between two senators of the same party, because they must share the same limelight, which these days means television time."[55]

Finally, there is the "compared to what?" syndrome. Press treatment of some senators is initially influenced by the degree of affection in which their predecessors were held. Charles Grassley thinks Senate reporters expected so little of him because he was taking the place of John Culver who was popular in the press galleries. On the other hand, the *San Francisco Chronicle*'s John Fogarty was just one of the California reporters who told me that Pete Wilson was being so well received because he is S. I. Hayakawa's replacement.

Senators become news—as opposed to merely being players in the drama of the Senate—when they run for president or otherwise get themselves into trouble. There were no Senate scandals in 1983, but one in 1984 illustrates how this genre gets played out in the national press. On July 23 Jack Anderson announced in his syndicated column:

> Sen. Mark O. Hatfield [R-Oregon], whose reelection effort this year is supported by peace and nuclear-freeze groups, has used his considerable influence to promote an oil pipeline project hatched by an international arms merchant.
> Hatfield, chairman of the Appropriations Committee, has continued his helpful efforts even after being warned that the Greek munitions dealer, Basil Tsakos, had a criminal record. . . . [56]

Another July 23 article in the *Washington Post*, by investigative reporter Howard Kurtz, confirmed that Hatfield had arranged meetings for Tsakos with the secretary of energy and the president

---

55. "After First Year, Evans' Senate Star Outshines Gorton's," *Longview Daily News* and other Washington state newspapers, September 16, 1984.
56. "Hatfield Helps Arms Dealer's Pipeline Project," *Washington Post*, July 23, 1984.

of Exxon and had endorsed the proposal to build a trans-Africa oil pipeline in conversations with the secretary of defense and the president of the Sudan. The article also disclosed that Tsakos had paid Hatfield's wife, Antoinette, $40,000 in real estate fees.[57] Hatfield said that there was no connection between his wife's real estate work for Tsakos and his support of the pipeline:

> "We have maintained very separate and distinct professional careers," Hatfield said. "She has not been involved in my political matters, and I really haven't been involved in her business."
> Hatfield said he has long been concerned that the United States is "very vulnerable to supply cutoffs in the Middle East" and faces "the great potential for a superpower confrontation" over Mideast oil. He said the pipeline could defuse the situation. . . . "That was my one and only interest in this," said Hatfield.

This was still the general outline of the story when it was concluded (in the short-term perspective of the media) on August 13 at a Portland, Oregon, press conference in which Hatfield said he had been "insensitive" to the appearance of conflict of interest, and his wife said that she would donate the money she had received from Tsakos to the Shriners Hospital for Crippled Children.[58] However, between the two dates the public learned a good deal about the Hatfields' finances, Tsakos's deals, and the pipeline project, as well as their thoughts on spousal rights and obligations.

A running story of this nature is usually constructed in modest increments. The actors are rarely forthcoming, and the news organizations are limited in time and resources. So events uncovered become a form of a soap opera; reporters need add only one interesting new fact to what was known yesterday for there to be another episode. Thus some of the lead paragraphs:

August 8
The Senate Ethics Committee has begun taking sworn testimony in an investigation into the relationship between Sen. Mark O. Hatfield and a Greek financier who paid Hatfield's wife $40,000 for what

---

57. "Hatfield Aided Greek Who Paid Real Estate Fee to Senator's Wife," *Washington Post*, July 23, 1984.

58. Howard Kurtz and Katharine Macdonald, "Hatfield Admits 'Error in Judgment,'" *Washington Post*, August 14, 1984.

the senator says were real estate services, according to informed sources.

August 9

Basil Tsakos, a Greek arms dealer who entangled Sen. Mark O. Hatfield and other Washington power brokers in a $15 billion trans-African oil pipeline scheme, was up to his collar in deals. For example, in February he tried to sell U.S.-made attack helicopters to the Iranian government from his Washington office in apparent violation of U.S. law, according to an intercepted cable.

August 10

When Sen. Mark O. Hatfield agreed to help Greek financier Basil A. Tsakos with plans to build a trans-African oil pipeline, he joined a long list of former government officials and corporate executives who were involved in the $12 billion project.

August 11

During a period when his wife, Antoinette Hatfield, was receiving payments from a Greek financier, Sen. Mark O. Hatfield was taking out more than half a dozen large personal loans and selling real estate, antiques, a coin collection and other personal property.

August 13

Two former employees of Greek financier Basil A. Tsakos have charged in sworn congressional testimony that Antoinette Hatfield, wife of Sen. Mark O. Hatfield . . . performed no services for the $40,000 she was paid by Tsakos and that the senator's account of her work is "a total fabrication."[59]

Each new "fact," of course, must be accompanied by a reiteration of what is already known. (A newspaper or news broadcast is constructed as if the reader or listener were learning about an event for the first time.) So news stories of a scandal grow exponentially until a denouement is reached, then suddenly end. Those who followed the Hatfield-Tsakos story in the *Washington Post* and *New York Times* (combined) would have been offered the

59. See Howard Kurtz, "Hatfield's Dealings with Pipeline Advocate Probed," *Washington Post*, August 8, 1984; Jack Anderson, "Weapons Dealer Tried to Make Iran a Customer," *Washington Post*, August 9, 1984; Howard Kurtz, "U.S. Officials Backed Off Tsakos Plan," *Washington Post*, April 10, 1984; Mary Thornton and Howard Kurtz, "Hatfield Was Borrowing, Selling Last Year," *Washington Post*, August 11, 1984; and Howard Kurtz, "Testimony Contradicts Hatfield," *Washington Post*, August 13, 1984.

following quantity of information (including headlines, photographs, and maps):

Date	Column inches	
July 23	38	(Jack Anderson breaks story)
August 8	70	
August 9	99	
August 13	131	
August 14	116	(Hatfield's press conference)
August 15	13	
Total (7/23-8/19)	728	

After Hatfield's press conference, the press concluded (correctly) that the senator's defense was sufficient to ensure his reelection. News organizations then reassigned reporters to other stories.

There were two other middling senatorial scandals in 1984. In May, Howard Metzenbaum reported receiving a $250,000 "finder's fee" for connecting the buyer and seller of the Hay-Adams Hotel across from the White House. The only illegality subsequently charged was that the Ohio senator may have violated a District of Columbia real estate regulation, but the District government eventually decided that he "did not act as a real estate broker or salesperson in the sale . . . [and] this matter merits no further action."[60] In June, Roger Jepsen confirmed a story that had been reported by a Dubuque radio station, saying, according to the Associated Press, "he had visited a sex club the year before his election because he mistakenly believed it was a health spa, despite a notice on a membership application that nude encounters were offered to members."[61]

The Iowa senator was decisively defeated in November, but neither his revelation nor Metzenbaum's were sustained national stories. The Washington press corps had never taken Jepsen seri-

60. Ann Mariano, "Metzenbaum Role in Hotel Sale Cleared," *Washington Post*, August 29, 1984.
61. "Visited Sex Club in Belief It Was Health Spa, Senator Says," *Los Angeles Times*, June 7, 1984.

ously—"a man whose Senate term has been dogged by embarrassing incidents and maladroit statements," according to the Wall Street Journal's Dennis Farney.[62] Metzenbaum, who is taken seriously, cut his political losses by almost instantly (unlike the Hatfields) returning the money and stating, "This was a legitimate business transaction and was openly reported on my financial disclosure. It was legal. It was ethical. However, I have been in public life long enough to know that reality and perception can be easily confused."[63]

When the Hastings Center was asked by the Senate Select Committee on Ethics to study possible revisions of the Senate code of official conduct, the center's scholars found that legislators brought "a measure of paranoia" to their perceptions of how the press covers questions of legislative ethics. However, they also concluded that the paranoia was not without cause, citing a CBS evening news broadcast on June 30, 1982, during which two teenage pages in the House of Representatives charged congressmen with involving them in homosexual affairs.[64] The boys eventually recanted their stories, and FBI investigations proved that the charges were unfounded.

If 1983 was a null year for congressional scandals, and 1984's scandals were small potatoes, the Capitol Hill scandals of 1980 were extraordinary by any standards. It was a year in which eleven present or former members of Congress faced criminal charges or went to prison. The main scandal resulted from Operation Abscam, with FBI agents masquerading as Arab sheiks and seven legislators (one of whom was a senator) becoming enmeshed in a web of bribes. In the House of Representatives there were also two homosexual scandals, one congressman censured for financial misconduct involving campaign funds, another resigning after he pleaded guilty to defrauding the government, and a committee chairman going to jail for taking payroll kickbacks. There were

62. "In Wake of Scandal, Sen. Jepsen Relies on 'Damage Control,' " Wall Street Journal, June 19, 1984.

63. "Metzenbaum to Return Fee," Washington Times, May 25, 1984.

64. Daniel Callahan, William Green, Bruce Jennings, and Martin Linsky, Congress and the Media: The Ethical Connection (The Hastings Center, Institute of Society, Ethics and the Life Sciences, 1985), pp. vi–vii, 7–8.

several lesser scandals as well.[65] According to Timothy Cook's study, 1980 was the year in which the "ethical accusations" variable was the biggest single determinant of which House member was mentioned on the evening network news programs and in the *New York Times*.[66]

Congressional scandals may happen less often than we imagine—perhaps because we tend to savour them much longer than the more mundane news from Washington—but their potential effects on politicians (including the innocent ones) add a sense of danger to the otherwise healthy relationship between the press and Congress. They are the unplanned and unexpected in the news-producing equation. They happen because there are law enforcement agencies, political opponents, and investigative reporters. They are, of course, the most unpleasant way for a legislator to make news.

The best way for a senator to be noticed by the national media is to run for president, or, if it is credible, to hint broadly of his or her availability for the job.

Nearly one of every four points in the 1983 national media rating system can be attributed to senators' being mentioned as presidential contenders. If John Glenn had not sought the Democratic presidential nomination, his ranking would have dropped from first to thirteenth. Alan Cranston would have gone from second to seventeenth, Gary Hart from fifth to eighteenth, and

65. The legislators caught by Abscam were Senator Harrison A. Williams, Jr. (D-N.J.), and Congressmen John W. Jenrette, Jr. (D-S.C.), Richard Kelly (R-Fla.), Raymond F. Lederer (D-Pa.), John M. Murphy (D-N.Y.), Michael (Ozzie) Myers (D-Pa.), and Frank Thompson, Jr. (D-N.J.). Another House member, John P. Murtha (D-Pa.), was named an unindicted coconspirator. The House members involved in homosexual scandals were Robert E. Bauman (R-Md.) and Jon C. Hinson (R-Miss.). Charles H. Wilson (D-Calif.) was the legislator censured by the House. Daniel J. Flood (D-Pa.) resigned after a conviction, and Charles C. Diggs, Jr. (D-Mich.) went to prison. Among other congressional scandals that were in the courts in 1980, Congressman Claude (Buddy) Leach (D-La.) was accused of vote buying, and former Congressman Charles J. Carney (D-Ohio) was charged with accepting an illegal gratuity during the period he had been in Congress. See *Congressional Quarterly Almanac*, vol. 36 (1980), pp. 513–26.

66. "Newsmakers, Lawmakers and Leaders," paper delivered at the 1984 annual meeting of the American Political Science Association (*Legislative Studies Quarterly*, forthcoming),, tables 7, 8.

Ernest Hollings would have fallen all the way from sixth to a forty-third-place tie with Delaware's William Roth. These four men accounted for 27 percent of all national coverage of senators in 1983, and 81 percent of their newsworthiness related to the race for the presidency.[67] (The impact of running for president has greater weight in national newspapers than on the television networks. The candidacies of Glenn, Cranston, Hart, and Hollings accounted for 12 percent of the Senate coverage on television evening news and 10 percent on the Sunday interview programs but 28 percent of the coverage by the five newspapers used for rating.)

Although the past two presidents have been ex-governors, the Senate is still the major launching pad for presidential contenders, especially in the Democratic party. The high-water mark was probably in early 1972 when ten senators—almost one-fifth of the Democrats—were being talked about as potential nominees.[68] Four—the number of senators who sought the presidency in 1984—is more typical. Moreover, senators who lose a presidential nomination often turn up on the ticket as the candidate for vice-president.[69]

The Great Mentioner, an illusive spirit who divines which politicians will be considered potential presidential nominees by the news media, is an invention of New York Times columnist Russell Baker. "Just why The Great Mentioner mentions some names and not others is very puzzling," notes the Washington Post's David S. Broder.[70] Still, we know that the official date to start mentioning—something like a political Groundhog Day—is exactly four years before the candidates are chosen.

67. There were also some presidential mentions for Edward Kennedy and Dale Bumpers.

68. The ten senators were Birch Bayh, Fred Harris, Harold Hughes, Hubert Humphrey, Vance Hartke, Henry Jackson, George McGovern, Edward Kennedy, Edmund Muskie, and William Proxmire.

69. This was the case with Estes Kefauver (1956), Lyndon Johnson (1960), and Edmund Muskie (1968); other senators who have been nominated for vice-president during this period include Hubert Humphrey (1964), Thomas Eagleton (1972), Walter Mondale (1976), and Bob Dole (1976).

70. "Political Reporters in Presidential Politics," in Charles Peters and Timothy J. Adams, eds., Inside the System (Praeger, 1970), p. 12.

Thus as Democratic convention delegates gathered in San Francisco in July 1984, reporters were busy writing stories about who might be nominated in 1988. The *Wall Street Journal* carried over the names of Edward Kennedy and Gary Hart from previous lists, added Bill Bradley and Dale Bumpers as hot prospects, and included Joseph Biden and Christopher Dodd as other possibilities. Sandy Grady of the Knight-Ridder Newspapers included Hart, Biden, Bradley, and Bumpers but discarded Kennedy as "a graying lion." U.S. *News & World Report* saw Hart threatened in 1988 by "a new crop of even younger politicians—such as Senators Bill Bradley, 40, of New Jersey and Joseph Biden, 41, of Delaware." *Time* quoted retiring Senator Paul Tsongas: "The entire stable of potential candidates for 1988 comes from the new Democratic group of politicians." The magazine then commented, "Bradley, Dodd and Joseph Biden of Delaware lead the new-generation Democrats in the Senate."[71]

That the press should have settled on Hart, Kennedy, Dodd, Bumpers, Biden, and Bradley is instructive and illustrates how the system works.

Every person who enters the Senate is placed on the political press corps' mental list of potential presidents. He or she then may be crossed off. Senators can be eliminated by being too old, too stupid, too shopworn, too provincial or state oriented, or too uninterested. Being uninterested usually means that a senator has chosen to make a career in the Senate. Daniel P. Moynihan, for example, used to be mentioned, but in recent years the New Yorker seems to have made it clear that he is no longer receptive to running for president. It is probable, too, that no Jews would be considered at this time, which is the reason to delete such names as Carl Levin, Arlen Specter, Rudy Boschwitz, and Warren Rudman. (There are presently no blacks or Hispanics in the Senate.) State size is no longer a factor; Senator George McGovern, the Democratic nominee in 1972, came from South Dakota.

If these criteria are applied to the list of Democrats in the 1983

71. Dennis Farney and David Rogers, "Rising Democrats," *Wall Street Journal*, July 18, 1984; Sandy Grady, "Kennedy's Punch Banks on Past," Columbia (S.C.) *State*, July 28, 1984; "Where Hart and Jackson Go From Here," U.S. *News & World Report* (July 23, 1984), p. 31; and "A Party in Search of Itself," *Time* (July 16, 1984), p. 20.

Senate, those who survive almost exactly correspond to the media's "early line" for 1988.[72] Yet several of these senators received only modest attention: Biden ranked thirty-third and Bradley was tied with three other senators in fifty-fourth place. They were not being mentioned for president because they generated massive publicity or had elaborate press operations. Indeed, the two senators have small, low-key press staffs. Bradley, it might be assumed, could afford to bide his time. He was a celebrity before he was a senator; his uniform (number 24) is on display at Madison Square Garden. But what of Biden? He was never famous. He would not be mistaken for a matinee idol. His remarks are articulate without being graceful. He seeks to be pleasant and helpful to reporters but only up to a point. "They probably know less about me than any other so-called national senator," he told me. "This is because I commute daily to Delaware. I don't live in Washington. So if 'The Today Show' wants me to be on the 7:10 segment I decline because I'd have to leave home at 4 a.m. It's the same for the late-night programs."

Rather, the Bradleys and the Bidens are mentioned for president because there will always be a list of potentials—a starting place for those who think about choosing candidates—and they have not yet been eliminated from it or removed themselves in terms that are taken at face value. But once on the list, their capacity for self-promotion increases arithmetically. This raises the question of whether the Senate is a good place from which to run for the White House.

Howard Baker obviously thinks not. In 1984, while serving as majority leader, he declined to seek reelection to the Senate. Yet at the same time, he told Wall Street Journal reporter Dennis Farney, "Let me say it flat out: If the Lord lets me stay healthy, and if there's any way at all to do it, I'm going to run [for President] in 1988."[73] The Tennessee Republican is following what has become

72. In the Republican party the "early line" consisted of Vice-President George Bush, Senators Howard Baker and Bob Dole, and Congressman Jack Kemp. However, the Great Mentioner never sleeps: a National Journal story on July 7, 1985, added Senators John Danforth, David Durenberger, John Heinz, and Richard Lugar, while the front page of the New York Times on August 20, 1985, found that Paul Laxalt "has long been regarded as a possible Presidential candidate in 1988."

73. "Baker is Ready for 'Civilian' Life," Wall Street Journal, August 8, 1984.

the conventional wisdom in high-stakes politics. The last three elected presidents—Richard Nixon, Jimmy Carter, and Ronald Reagan—were unemployed in politics at the time of their elections. This suggests that successfully running for a presidential nomination takes full-time and undivided attention. At least so it appears to political junkies, who, like generals, fight the last war. As for Gary Hart's future prospects, the authoritative *National Journal* wrote before the 1984 election, "If Mondale is not elected, many in Colorado believe that Hart will pass up the Senate to remove any distractions in the way of another long march for the Presidency."[74] And as expected, Mondale lost and Hart announced on January 4, 1986, that he was not going to stand for reelection in November. His press secretary explained that he "didn't feel he could go to the voters and ask for another term when running for president was a live option."[75] Running for president from the Senate, however, most often hinders the candidate who also holds a leadership position—such as Lyndon Johnson, Hubert Humphrey, and Henry Jackson; other senators who have been backbenchers at the time they sought nomination—John Kennedy, Barry Goldwater, George McGovern—have had a higher success rate in recent years.[76]

Although many reasons could be given for leaving the Senate as the best path to the presidency, lack of publicity is not one of them.[77] Hart and Glenn—and even Cranston and Hollings (both of whom complained that the press was not noticing them)—got a great deal of media attention and probably much more than if they had not had the Senate as a platform in 1983. This, of course, might be a problem, as David S. Broder will argue in a forthcoming

74. Ronald Brownstein, "What Lies Ahead for Gary Hart?" *National Journal Convention Special*, July 21, 1984.

75. Paul West, "Looking to '88, Hart passes up third Senate term," Baltimore *Sun*, January 5, 1986.

76. See Richard E. Cohen, "As a Launching Pad for Presidency, Congress Isn't What It Used To Be," *National Journal*, vol. 12 (March 8, 1980), p. 400.

77. A senator might pass up a race for reelection because of the possibility of losing and because of the financial cost. See Paul Taylor, "Hart Campaign Back to Source," *Washington Post*, May 8, 1984; and T. R. Reid, "Hart Knows Lines, But Not Plot," *Washington Post*, August 14, 1985. Then, too, there are times when being perceived by the public as a "Washington insider" is a drawback in seeking the presidency.

book. Candidates may benefit from the early inattention of the national press corps. A "long period of relative obscurity," he contends, enables the candidates "to test their themes and practice their speeches without . . . fly-specking close scrutiny by the press." Relatedly, Greg Schneiders, who was John Glenn's communications director, has said, "It's the taking a stand on every issue that kills you in the Senate."

Still, Hart, Cranston, Glenn, and Hollings did not lose the 1984 nomination because they were U.S. Senators. And if they had left the Senate, they still would not have been nominated. As journalists and scholars have noted, the Senate remains the great presidential incubator.[78]

78. See Robert L. Peabody, Norman J. Ornstein, and David W. Rohde, "The United States Senate as a Presidential Incubator: Many Are Called But Few Are Chosen," *Political Science Quarterly*, vol. 91 (Summer 1976).

V

Courting the Media

BOB DOLE was one of the national media's favorite senators in 1983. He was the chairman of the Finance Committee. He was closely associated with important issues, notably reform of the social security system. He made it clear that he would seek the Republican presidential nomination if Ronald Reagan chose not to run for reelection. He was witty and articulate, with the reputation of being able to supply a quotable quip for any occasion (at Elizabeth Dole's confirmation hearing: "I regret that I have but one wife to give for my country's infrastructure").[1] But for all the characteristics that would seem to make him a natural media star, Dole probably worked harder at attracting national coverage than any other member of the Senate. He was a classic example of the overachiever in terms of courting the media.

Despite Dole's advantages, publicity was not automatic in 1983. Of the six media leaders that year, four were Democrats actively running for president and one was the majority leader (the ultimate insider, who meets with reporters daily when the Senate is in session). Dole's platform—the Finance Committee—does not

---

1. Alan Ehrenhalt, ed., *Politics in America*, 1984 (CQ Press, 1983), p. 552. Also see Jonathan Fuerbringer, "From Barb to Quip, Dole Leads With His Wit," *New York Times*, November 30, 1984.

rate as many network cameras as a lot of other committees (see table 3-1).

Like the other senators who must work hard to see themselves on television or their names in headlines, Dole fed the news machines by issuing press releases. by holding press conferences, by making speeches, by being accessible to reporters. In 1983, according to a Common Cause report, he gave more than 120 speeches for which he received fees (he contributed much of this income to charity).[2] He was also at or near the top on the other scales I have devised to gauge the effort factor, that is, the output that is expended in calling attention to oneself.[3]

Table 5-1 represents three types of activities whose purpose is to be noticed. The left column ranks each senator who sent at least fifty press releases to the Senate's radio and television gallery (April 1983 through March 1984); the middle column ranks each senator who was interviewed more than eleven times in the gallery's studio (January 1983 through June 1984); the right column ranks all senators who had more than five scheduled news conferences at the Capitol other than in their own offices (July 1983 to June 1984). Those senators who were seeking reelection in 1984 are less likely to appear in the table than if they had been sampled in other years—reelection campaigns will wondrously focus senators' attention on their states' local press corps. Indeed, senators who are about to face the voters do not spend as much time in Washington.[4] Linda Hill, press secretary for Armed Services Committee Chairman John Tower, said that had her boss not chosen to retire in 1984, "the Lubbock [Texas] press would have taken on more importance than

2. "Senator Dole's Personal Income Tax Information," undated 1984 press release, office of Robert Dole; and Common Cause press releases, May 15 and May 25, 1984.

3. Senator Dole was also among twenty-three senators (eleven Republicans, twelve Democrats) who provided me with a complete set of their press releases for 1984. The average number of releases was 104; Dole was the leader with 260.

4. Of the thirty-three senators whose terms were about to expire in 1984, only seven are listed in table 5-1. For the increased number of trips that senators make to their home states in the years that they seek reelection, see Richard F. Fenno, Jr., *The United States Senate: A Bicameral Perspective* (American Enterprise Institute, 1982), pp. 33–35.

Table 5-1. *Senator Media Activities, 1983-84*

Press releases		TV studio interviews[a]		News conferences	
Dole, R. (R-Kans.)	120	Tsongas, P. (D-Mass.)	26	Kennedy, E. (D-Mass.)	15
Hatch, O. (R-Utah)	115	Mathias, C. (R-Md.)	23	Cranston, A. (D-Calif.)	13
Hart, G. (D-Colo.)	108	Pressler, L. (R-S.D.)	21	Dole, R. (R-Kans.)	9
Kennedy, E. (D-Mass.)	106	Dole, R. (R-Kans.)	21	Durenberger, D. (R-Minn.)	8
Proxmire, W. (D-Wis.)	83	Cranston, A. (D-Calif.)	20	Danforth, J. (R-Mo.)	8
Cranston, A. (D-Calif.)	78	Hart, G. (D-Colo.)	20	Hart, G. (D-Colo.)	8
Wilson, P. (R-Calif.)	78	Leahy, P. (D-Vt.)	18	Hawkins, P. (R-Fla.)	8
Hollings, E. (D-S.C.)	72	Levin, C. (D-Mich.)	18	Packwood, B. (R-Oreg.)	8
Byrd, R. (D-W.Va.)	70	Weicker, L. (R-Conn.)	18	Chiles, L. (D-Fla.)	7
Stevens, T. (R-Alaska)	66	Metzenbaum, H. (D-Ohio)	17	D'Amato, A. (R-N.Y.)	7
Quayle, D. (R-Ind.)	63	Chiles, L. (D-Fla.)	17	Mathias, C. (R-Md.)	7
Packwood, B. (R-Oreg.)	59	Biden, J. (D-Del.)	15	Metzenbaum, H. (D-Ohio)	7
Percy, C. (R-Ill.)	55	Kasten, R. (R-Wis.)	15	Byrd, R. (D-W.Va.)	6
Roth, W. (R-Del.)	54	Nunn, S. (D-Ga.)	15	Dodd, C. (D-Conn.)	6
Grassley, C. (R-Iowa)	53	Hatch, O. (R-Utah)	14	Kasten, R. (R-Wis.)	6
Levin, C. (D-Mich.)	52	Dodd, C. (D-Conn.)	13	Riegle, D. (D-Mich.)	6
Helms, J. (R-N.C.)	51	Hollings, E. (D-S.C.)	12		

a. In theory, a senator is supposed to be invited by a reporter to come to the studio for an interview; in practice, a press secretary can always ask a reporter to extend an invitation.

the national press, and it would have been the national reporters who would have had a hard time getting ahold of Tower."

Some very visible senators—Daniel P. Moynihan, John Tower, Paul Laxalt, Barry Goldwater, Mark Hatfield, and Dale Bumpers—are not to be found in any column of table 5-1. Jesse Helms barely shows up (fifty-one press releases). Obviously senators do not get noticed strictly by wooing national reporters. Most of their press operations are directed at the local media.[5] During the year that I camped out with the press in the Senate, only six senators' press secretaries regularly "worked the galleries," that is showed up at least several times a week to chat with reporters. As one of these veterans noted, "It can be a scary place for the typical press secretary who won't know many of the reporters." Alan Cranston was the only senator I interviewed who credited his press secretary (Murray Flander) as one of the reasons why he made news; at the other extreme, William Proxmire told me that "press secretaries are useless" (he is one of two senators who do not have a press secretary). The truth probably lies between these polar positions. Some press secretaries are said to have made a substantial difference to their bosses' reputations. James Brady, who later served President Reagan, is often cited on Capitol Hill for his service to Senator William Roth. A 1979 article in the *Washington Journalism Review* claimed, "Regardless of his effectiveness in serving his constituents, Bill Roth came to Congress with two strikes against him: he was a Republican, and he was from Delaware. Now, thanks to Brady, Bill Roth has influence, Bill Roth is news and, when reporters go looking for reaction to a Presidential message, they know they can always count on Bill Roth (and Jim Brady) to deliver the goods."[6] However, the more typical press secretary in the Senate does not stay long enough to be said to have real impact. Of all the senators' press secretaries who were on the job at the start of the Ninety-eighth Congress in January 1983, about 41 percent had

5. Timothy E. Cook documents the same conclusion in a study of members' press operations in the House of Representatives. See "Marketing the Members: the Ascent of the Congressional Press Secretary," paper delivered at the 1985 annual meeting of the Midwest Political Science Association.

6. Adrian C. Taylor, "The Flacks on the Hill," *Washington Journalism Review*, vol. 1 (June/July, 1979), p. 37.

left by the time the next Congress convened in January 1985.[7]

There is no way of knowing where a Dole or a Hatch or a Cranston would have been located in the 1983 national media ranking had they fired their press secretaries and refused to answer reporters' calls. (Immediately off the Senate floor is an ornate room, called the President's Room, to which a reporter can summon a senator for an interview. Paul Houston, of the Los Angeles Times, told me in 1984 that only two senators, Robert Byrd and Barry Goldwater, have left instructions that they will not take reporters' requests to leave the floor. The loudspeaker in the press gallery announces, "Mr. Domenici is in the President's Room and is available if any reporter wishes to see him.") My own guess is that making an effort, as reflected in table 5-1, could move a senator to a high middle rating—about the placement of a Pete Wilson or a Charles Grassley—but no higher unless the senator also has a leadership position or is known to want to run for president.

As we walked across the Capitol grounds on a brisk early spring day in 1984, I asked Martin Tolchin, the New York Times correspondent who then specialized in the Senate, how many senators' press secretaries he could name. He named thirteen. Warming to the game, he went to a list of senators in the press gallery and with this aid was able to add another ten names to his list—for a total of twenty-three out of one hundred. The press secretaries known to Tolchin represented senators (in almost three equal parts) who were key leaders, or were from the Times' circulation area, or had been elected in interesting campaigns. The lesson that he drew from this exercise was that press secretaries are not very important to him in doing his job. But possibly another lesson could be that from the point of view of a national reporter most senators make very little news. (Also, some senators' press secretaries, knowing how difficult it is to get on network news, do not encourage their bosses to make the effort: to try and fail might be thought to reflect badly on a press secretary's ability.)

7. The 41 percent represents thirty-seven of ninety press secretaries. This, of course, excludes those who worked for senators who had died, retired, been defeated, or who did not have press secretaries.

What happens if we turn the effort factor upside down, looking now at those senators who do not send their releases to the TV gallery, do not get interviewed in its studio, and do not call press conferences? In 1983, three senators had a zero rating—Edward Zorinsky, Spark Matsunaga, and Quentin Burdick. Frank Murkowski rated 1 (a press release); Thad Cochran, Paul Trible, Chic Hecht, Howell Heflin, and Wendell Ford rated 3 points; Don Nickles, 4; James Abdnor and Walter Huddleston, 5; David Boren, 6; and James Exon, 7. These senators were among the under-achievers.

Those on the lower end of the Senate's national media scale are an odd admixture in terms of why they stay out of the limelight. The underachievers include the too old, too new, too scared, too provincial, too stupid, and too uninterested. Some members fit in more than one category.

In 1965–66, 1969–70, and 1973–74, John Stennis ranked comfortably within the top third of the Senate in appearances on the Associated Press wires. For most of the time, he was chairman of the Armed Services Committee. But by 1983 he was eighty-two years old; his national media score was 8 (compared to John Glenn's 563). Some senators slow down, yet getting old is not by itself an explanation. Stennis was born in 1901, Strom Thurmond and Jennings Randolph in 1902. Thurmond (media score: 28; ranking 41) had an energetic press secretary and still seemed attentive to the news media; Randolph (media score: 9; ranking: 78) ranked eighty-third in 1969–70. The West Virginia Democrat had been an anonymous younger senator and an anonymous old senator.

Being new to the Senate may also be a factor in underachieving. Charles Mathias is a good example of a senator who has slowly gained in media notice without benefit of a major committee chairmanship or of being viewed as a presidential contender. Mathias was elected to the Senate in 1968, and, as one can chart from the data in appendix B, he ranked fifty-sixth in 1969, thirty-third in 1973, and thirteenth in 1983. While the rise could be partly attributed to his move toward maverick status, there are reporters who believe that it also reflects intellectual growth; they consider Mathias to be a wiser and more interesting figure than he used to be.

No doubt.some of 1983's underachievers will move up in newsworthiness as they gain seniority. New Mexico's Jeff Bingaman, elected in 1982, "is a quiet man, regarded as very smart and marked as a comer by many observers," according to Pat Towell of the *Congressional Quarterly*.[8] New Hampshire's Warren Rudman, elected in 1980, "is a long distance runner, willing to accommodate other senators, and apt to be a future [Senate] leader," said the *Manchester Union Leader*'s Tom Gorey in 1984.

Some media underachievers seem to choose such a role. Daniel Inouye's trend line shows a senator who prefers to keep a low profile while at the same time rising in influence among his colleagues. As the secretary of the Democratic Conference, he is the third-ranking Democrat in the Senate. According to Martin Tolchin, "He has a reputation as a persuasive, Lyndon Johnson-style, one-on-one legislator, close to the center of power."[9] As such, Inouye can adjust his publicity to the needs of his personality. But his pattern also reflects a senator with a safe seat and no presidential aspirations; he simply does not need the volume of publicity that others may require. Still, there were only six Senate leaders in the bottom third on the national news scale, and all were in the minority party. If a senator wishes to stay out of sight, it is obviously easier when his party is out of power.

Several senators near the bottom of the 1983 media ranking have a history of trying to draw attention to themselves, but the reporters in the press galleries have learned to dismiss their efforts as headline hunting. As Joseph Nocera said of a 1977 statement by Edward Zorinsky (D-Nebraska):

> Zorinsky announced to a *Washington Star* reporter that the Senate was a mess, that he didn't think it could ever get anything done, and therefore he had seriously considered quitting to find another line of work. . . . [I]t was the lead story of the night. That's the important thing. Nor did it make much difference that Zorinsky never really meant it (he had, in fact, made the whole thing up)—that is something other quality headline hunters could understand and sympa-

8. "Armed Services Panel: Goldwater in the Cockpit," *Congressional Quarterly Weekly Report*, vol. 43 (February 16, 1985), p. 300.

9. "Inouye's Orchids for Israel," *New York Times*, March 4, 1985.

thize with. The man needed a quick fix and was willing to do just about anything to get it.[10]

The largest category of underachievers is the provincials, those senators who see their jobs as almost totally concerned with local representation. Perhaps half the bottom third fit this description. In a sense they act as House members on a somewhat grander scale. The classic case is Democrat Quentin Burdick of North Dakota, who has been in the Senate since 1960 and whose passion for anonymity was once a laugh line in Mark Russell's nightclub routine. The provincials rarely make statements about national matters and therefore do not get national attention. They are not necessarily men of small egos, however. In August 1984 I joined Alan Dixon, freshman Democratic senator from Illinois, in the Capitol broadcast studio for a screening of a "town meeting" that he had recently taped for a Peoria cable broadcaster. Dixon was delighted with himself as he watched his answers to constituents' questions. "I got out of that pretty good," he noted after a delicate response, and laughed heartily. For this senator, who told me he was "a state man," happiness was apparently how it plays in Peoria. "I've won twenty-nine of twenty-nine elections, so I must be doing something right," he said.

"It is a rare Congressman who is not anxious to have his thoughts and actions reported in all areas of the communications media," wrote Joseph Clark when he was a senator from Pennsylvania,[11] and if all the senators, scholars, and journalists who report that publicity is the mother's milk of politicians are correct, there must be a lot of incompetent senators in terms of making national news. Such claims, however, should not be accepted without qualification. There are some senators who do not want national media attention because they see the dangers of publicity as outweighing its virtues. William S. Cohen (R-Maine), in a diary of his first year in the Senate in 1979, commented with regard to Maine's other senator,

> I had learned from [Edmund Muskie's] experiences some lessons about the national press. Washington is the most transient city in

10. "How to Make the Front Page," *Washington Monthly* (October 1978), pp. 14–15.

11. *Congress: The Sapless Branch* (Harper & Row, 1964), p. 75.

the world. Not all of the flotsam is in the Potomac. Even in banana republics the powerful do not rise and sink with such regularity. Politicians need publicity to survive, but one runs a serious risk in inviting close press scrutiny.[12]

Perhaps Cohen was thinking about the attacks on Muskie's wife in 1972 when he was seeking the Democratic presidential nomination.[13] Although these attacks came from the *Union Leader* of Manchester, New Hampshire, not from the national press corps, there is no doubt that the private lives, families, and friends of public persons are more and more considered newsworthy. And there are other costs associated with publicity. Michael J. Robinson and Kevin R. Appel, in a study of "Congress stories" on television network news in January and February 1976, could not find a single item that cast members of Congress in a positive light, and a small number —14 percent— that they felt were negative.[14] Also, remember Frank Church? George McGovern? Birch Bayh? J. William Fulbright? There is a list of senators who are said to have received so much national attention that they opened themselves to opponents' charges of losing touch with the people in their states.

Some states, however, seem to bask in the reflected glory of their national senators. For more than thirty years, Georgia sent Walter George to the Senate, where he chaired the Foreign Relations Committee; Georgia's Richard Russell served almost forty years and chaired the Armed Services Committee; and now Sam Nunn of Georgia is the ranking Democrat on Armed Services. Paul Wieck, the Washington correspondent for the *Albuquerque Journal*, says that his state similarly takes pride in producing national figures, and commenting on the reelection chances of a "locally oriented senator" who turned into a national senator, *Congressional Quarterly* correctly forecast in 1984 that "Domenici's stature in Washington has made him stronger in New Mexico."[15]

12. *Roll Call: One Year in the United States Senate* (Simon and Schuster, 1981), p. 161.
13. See Theodore H. White, *The Making of the President* 1972 (Atheneum, 1973), pp. 81–82.
14. "Network News Coverage of Congress," *Political Science Quarterly*, vol. 94 (Fall 1979), p. 412.
15. *Congressional Quarterly Weekly Report*, vol. 42 (February 25, 1984), p. 397.

What are the real risks of a senator's getting too much national attention? In the elections of 1954, 1966, 1970, 1974, and 1984, a total of fourteen incumbents were defeated; eight of them were highly visible and six were not. In 1984, when three senators lost their bids for reelection, one (Charles Percy) was in the top third, another (Roger Jepsen) the middle third, and the third (Walter D. Huddleston) the bottom third in media exposure. Still, it is likely that journalists will mainly recall that the voters rejected Percy, the chairman of the Foreign Relations Committee, not that they also rejected an obscure senator from Kentucky. From the evidence, it is about as difficult to conclude that too much national media exposure causes defeat as that too little causes victory. But the myth of the higher rate of defeat for national senators will persist, perhaps because, as I will argue in the last chapter, there is a growing industry that has to believe that the national news media have an effect—one way or another.

VI

Shrinking the Senate

SENATOR ALAN CRANSTON addressed an orientation session for freshman senators on November 30, 1982. According to his reading
text, typed for him in capital letters, he began,

> GOOD RELATIONS BETWEEN SENATORS AND THE PRESS DE-
> PEND IN LARGE PART ON THE EXTENT TO WHICH EACH OF THE
> PARTIES GETS WHAT HE WANTS FROM THE RELATIONSHIP.
> I THINK IT'S SAFE TO ASSUME THAT WHAT SENATORS—LIKE
> MOST PUBLIC FIGURES—WANT FROM THE PRESS IS COVERAGE.
> LOTS OF COVERAGE.

It should be a given, of course, that all senators want lots of
coverage in their states' newspapers and on their local radio and
television stations. But what of national media attention? Coverage may be what Democratic Whip Cranston wants (he ranked
second in 1983), yet one conclusion of this study is that national
coverage is not universally sought after by his colleagues.

Linda Peek is director of communications for the Democratic
Policy Committee of the Senate. It is her job to get Democratic
senators to speak on national issues for the national press. She
admitted to feeling frustrated in 1984. "Last week I wanted a
senator to go head-to-head with Reagan on the budget. 'The
President's forty points more popular than I am in my state,' he

said and refused." Peek now thinks "the Senate is primarily a local place designed for local consumption." Another staff member who has been a regular attendee of the Democratic senators' weekly caucus calls them "pathetic" sessions. "All they talk about is local politics or Senate politics, such as 'Don't make us vote on that or it will kill me.' " This is powerfully strange. Under the Constitution, senators are given long terms—six years, or four years longer than House members—and senators must be older. The reasons for the differences, according to *Federalist Paper* number 62, have to do with "the nature of senatorial trust; which, requiring greater extent of information and stability of character, requires at the same time, that the senator should have reached a period of life most likely to supply these advantages. . . . "[1] The Senate, in other words, was designed to be a body that would think deeply on great questions, "a worthy monument of the wisdom and foresight" of the founding fathers, concluded Lord Bryce.[2]

The Senate's new provincialism—if that is what it is—must be examined in the context of recent electoral history, for senators, above all else, are politicians. Every even-numbered year a third of the Senate must stand for reelection: in 1976, twelve Senate seats switched from one party to the other and eight senators were defeated; in 1978 there were again twelve party turnovers and eight defeated incumbents; in 1980, twelve seats again changed party and twelve incumbents lost either primaries or general elections. Moreover, in 1980 and 1982 twenty-one senators won by 52 percent of the vote or less.

Where are the safe Senate seats of yesteryear? Mostly gone. The

1. Max Beloff, ed., *The Federalist, or the New Constitution* (Basil Blackwell, 1948), p. 315. There is a certain irony here that scholars and journalists are beginning to write about. As the Senate becomes more like the House of Representatives, the House of Representatives is also becoming more like the Senate. Part of the cause again can be attributed to election prospects. Senate seats, as noted in this chapter, have become less safe, while, at the same time, House incumbents are now rarely defeated. Elliott Abrams, then a senator's administrative assistant, wrote, "One can plausibly argue that today the main differences between the House and the Senate are the Senate's smaller number of rules and greater number of presidential aspirants." See his "The Senate Since Yesterday," *American Spectator*, vol. 11 (February 1978), p. 12.

2. James Bryce, *The American Commonwealth* (Macmillan, 1922), vol. 1, p. 113.

United States has become a nation of two nearly equal political parties.[3]

Still, Wyoming is safe for Republicans. At a time in 1984 when the state's freshman Senator Alan Simpson, a candidate for re-election, was leading the fight to change the immigration law, a very prickly issue, political consultant David Keene commented, "Senators from small western states are the only ones still able to act like [national] senators." As if in confirmation, Donald Riegle, from the highly competitive state of Michigan, who came to the Senate in 1976 with national aspirations, told me that he now keeps half his professional staff in the state and is more interested in being noticed by the *Detroit News* than by the national press. For those legislators consumed with thoughts of their next election campaign, the national press corps may be viewed as a potential danger or as merely a distraction.

Priorities may change, of course, if the election dynamic changes. While eighteen freshmen senators were elected in 1976, twenty in 1978, and eighteen in 1980, the number dropped to five in 1982 (based on two defeats and three retirements) and seven in 1984 (three defeats, four retirements). Utah's Jake Garn told me in pungent language that he thinks more senators will be voluntarily retiring as the job frustrations continue to grow.[4] Much depends

3. The history of five elections—1976 through 1984—is that thirty-three states have replaced a senator of one party with a senator of the other party at least once—twice in Indiana, Minnesota, New Hampshire, and South Dakota; three times in Iowa. After the 1984 elections, Thomas E. Cavanagh and James L. Sundquist concluded, "For the first time since 1934 the country may now have a well-balanced, competitive-two-party system at the national level instead of the one-and-one-half party system it has known since the great realignment of the New Deal era." See their "The New Two-Party System" in John E. Chubb and Paul E. Peterson, eds., *The New Direction in American Politics.* (Brookings, 1985), p. 34.

4. See *contra*, Rich Burkhardt, "Decrease in Retirees Not Running for Other Offices," *Roll Call*, October 4, 1984, who argues that the number of "retirements will probably be low for several years to come." This is because most members have been in the Senate for less than ten years, "and are just now beginning to work into positions of authority," while historically retirees are usually senior senators. However, as of January 1986 seven senators had already indicated that they would not seek reelection in 1986, and only one of them, Barry Goldwater was over seventy years of age. The retirees are Goldwater (76), Russell Long (66), Paul Laxalt (63), Charles Mathias (63), Thomas Eagleton (56), John East (54), and Gary Hart (49).

on how well the Class of 1980 does at the polls in 1986. If the mortality rate stays low for three successive elections, we might suppose that more senators will home in less exclusively on local concerns.[5] But for the moment at least, there must be between a fourth and a third of the Senate who tend to avoid the national limelight and have deservedly earned the disinterest of national reporters.

Yet for those who do want lots of coverage by the national media, this study shows that it is not as easy to come by as previous commentators seem to have assumed. NBC producers are not forming a line on the right, Wall Street Journal reporters on the left. Part of the reason is access. Congressional reporters have it to a degree that is unheard of at the White House or the State Department, as illustrated in my diary entry of April 10, 1984:[6]

> The scene is the second floor hallway near the elevators outside of the Senate chamber. It is a favorite place for reporters to hang out. I am talking to a network correspondent when Senator Pell comes along. (He is the ranking Democrat on the Foreign Relations Committee.) Fearing that I am keeping the reporter from her work, I suggest that she might wish to interrupt our conversation. The reporter shrugs and continues talking. Other senators wait for the elevators—Thurmond, Sasser, Bradley, Packwood, Kasten—but none of the reporters I am with feel the need to ask them any questions. A Time correspondent says he is only here to try to catch Ted Kennedy.

My notes for that day read, "these reporters are almost blasé about their sources; there are, after all, so many of them." The typical senator is a supplicant to the television networks, which is why the networks are so unpopular on Capitol Hill.

The most startling statistic from the 1983 national media ranking remains: ten senators garnered 50 percent of the total score.

---

5. Press predictions, however, are that the twenty-two Republican seats at stake will suffer from the in-party's traditional midterm falloff. A representative article on 1986 Senate races from a mid-1985 perspective is Richard E. Cohen, "Laxalt Move Draws New Line in Senate Battle," National Journal, vol. 17 (August 8, 1985), p. 1949; also see Rhodes Cook, "Will the 'Six-Year Itch' Strike Again in 1986?" Congressional Quarterly Weekly Report, vol. 43 (June 29, 1985), pp. 1284–86.

6. Also see Bill Hogan, "The Congressional Correspondent," Washington Journalism Review, vol. 3 (June 1981), p. 35.

Or, ninety-one senators divided the other half, mostly in small individual servings.

Nor can the process be forced for those in a hurry. A good press operation makes relatively little difference; an agreeable personality makes even less difference. (When I asked a lunchroom table of reporters to name their favorite senators—favorite defined as those they would like to have as friends—the names offered were almost totally different from a previous survey of which senators reporters most liked to interview. Two reporters even talked of friendship with Quentin Burdick, the quintessentially invisible senator.) Senators who get ahead of their class usually do so on a temporary basis by taking a leadership position on a particular issue; when the issue is resolved, they must step back into rank.

It might be argued that the focus of the national press on a few Senate leaders is part of a conspiracy, the result of an old-boy network in which senior senators favor senior correspondents with information and senior correspondents flatter senior senators in print. Indeed, David S. Broder recalls something on this order when he was a young reporter:

> When I came to Washington [in the mid-1950s], there was a seniority system at work in the Senate press gallery almost as rigid as that of the Senate itself. A few minutes before the start of each day's session, the Majority Leader, Lyndon B. Johnson, and the Minority Leader, Everett McKinley Dirksen, would hold separate press conferences at their desks on the Senate floor. The reporters would gather around them in a semicircle, the senior correspondents in the inner ring, lesser ones to the back. Johnson and Dirksen were two of the great orators of their times, with lungs and throats that could fill an auditorium without a microphone. But at these press conferences, neither would raise his voice above the level of the boudoir; it was all whispered intimacies to the familiar friends in the front row. The rest of us learned what it was proper for us to know when a bell signaling the start of the session ended the press conferences and our elders relayed to us what they thought we should share.[7]

In 1984 when reporters gathered at the Senate desks of Howard Baker and Robert Byrd, it would have been impossible to sort out the oldtimers from the newcomers. Equality and rotation have caught up with the press corps; there are very few oldtimers

7. David S. Broder, untitled (Simon and Schuster, forthcoming).

among national correspondents. Steve Gerstel of UPI, Phil Jones of CBS, and UPI radio's Pye Chamberlayne are exceptions, not the rule. (Oldtimers in the Senate's press gallery are most likely regional correspondents representing newspapers in Baton Rouge or Milwaukee or Albuquerque.) Today, Broder notes, "journalists tend to be gypsies."

If, as Alan Cranston has said, "good relations between senators and the press depend in large part on the extent to which each of the parties gets what he wants from the relationship," what is it that reporters want? An easy question. Good stories. Especially stories that can be written in the time and space that journalists are given.[8] And this is another reason why the national press corps has unilaterally reduced the size of the Senate from one hundred to about twenty, although it is not always the same twenty. (Surely a senator with a point score in the 1983 media ranking of less than 50 can hardly be said to have been covered in the national press.)

The national press corps has always paid more attention to the Senate than to the House of Representatives. There is no lack of proof.[9] This is even true during periods—such as the present—when the House of Representatives is the body in opposition to the president.[10] Richard Fenno has claimed that such attention is a manifestation of an "all-encompassing pro-senator bias on the part of the media."[11] The Senate has the constitutional right to reject a president's treaties and a president's nominees, appealing prospects to a press corps that loves controversy. The Senate is also the incubator of presidential candidates who are then automatically newsworthy. But, most important, there are almost four-and-a-half times as many House members as there are senators.

8. On routinization as a central component of newsmaking, see Gaye Tuchman, *Making News: A Study in the Construction of Reality* (Free Press, 1978).

9. Susan H. Miller, "News Coverage of Congress: The Search for the Ultimate Spokesman," *Journalism Quarterly*, vol. 54 (Autumn 1977), pp. 461–62; Michael J. Robinson and Kevin R. Appel, "Network News Coverage of Congress," *Political Science Quarterly*, vol. 94 (Fall 1979), pp. 410–11; Stephen Hess, *The Washington Reporters*, pp. 101–02; and Timothy E. Cook, "Newsmakers, Lawmakers and Leaders," *Legislative Studies Quarterly* (forthcoming).

10. Foote and Weber, "Network Evening News Visibility," p. 3.

11. *The United States Senate: A Bicameral Perspective* (American Enterprise Institute, 1982), pp. 11–12.

As philosopher David Sidorsky notes, the goal of journalists is to transpose "an inherently ambiguous and complex event into a short narrative that can be simply told, have a central plot and retain the interest of the reader or viewer."[12] It is easier and faster to build a coherent story with a smaller cast of characters. The House of Representatives is too much like *War and Peace*; the Senate is more on the scale of *Crime and Punishment*.

Despite claims to the contrary, the introduction of television has not altered the pattern of coverage. The media's focus on a handful of senators is the same now as it was in 1953. Indeed, network television must be more exclusionary because it has a smaller newshole than newspapers, and it puts more emphasis on the articulateness of its interviewees. (The print media exclude the powerless; the electronic media exclude the powerless and the inarticulate.) The notion that national television would open up Senate coverage to a lot of marginal members should have been disproved by this collection of data.

Why the national media choose to cover certain senators and not others has been a central question of this study. The move away from junior senators, mavericks, and others, may be merely a reflection of what in social science terms is a small n. When a Robert F. Kennedy or a Daniel P. Moynihan enters the Senate, they are immediately newsworthy because they have been newsworthy before they were senators. But fewer new senators seem to be bringing national reputations with them to Washington. In terms of previous government experience, Alfonse D'Amato had been presiding supervisor for Hempstead, Long Island; Paula Hawkins had been a member of the Florida Public Service Commission; Joseph Biden was on the New Castle, Delaware, County Council; Dennis DeConcini had served as attorney for Pima County, Arizona; and Patrick Leahy held the same position in Chittenden County, Vermont. Mack Mattingly, Rudy Boschwitz, and Frank Lautenberg were businessmen who had never held elective office. Gordon Humphrey was an airline pilot. John East was a professor at East Carolina University. Orrin Hatch practiced

12. Joshua Muravchik, ed., *Perceptions of Israel in the American Media* (New York: American Jewish Committee, 1985), p. 9.

law in Salt Lake City, and David Durenberger was a St. Paul lawyer. Lawton Chiles, Sam Nunn, Walter Huddleston, Don Nickles, Malcolm Wallop, Bob Packwood, and Chic Hecht went from the state legislature to the U.S. Senate. I do not intend to imply that these people are not good senators, merely that it takes the Washington press corps longer to notice them.

But there is a good deal more to it than this. Part of the story goes back to 1950 and Joseph McCarthy, even though this predates the careers of almost all the reporters who presently cover the Senate. On the evening of February 9, 1950, in a speech before the Ohio County Women's Republican Club in Wheeling, West Virginia, Senator McCarthy, a first-term Republican from Wisconsin, announced, "I have here in my hand a list of 205" communists in the State Department. A charge of such magnitude and subsequent unsubstantiated accusations were objectively (*verbatim et literatim*) reported in the press. Edwin R. Bayley, Douglass Cater, and others have since pointed out that McCarthy created McCarthyism by using the conventions of the press just as a judo expert uses the strength of his opponent.[13] As Cater said, " 'Straight' news, the absolute commandment of most mass media journalism, had become a straitjacket. . . . "[14] The press learns primarily from its own mistakes. The reaction to its role in the McCarthy era, still a subliminal force in journalism, restrains congressional reporters from easily accepting "straight news" from those who have not earned their bona fides in the eyes of the press gallery.

Ann Compton, an experienced ABC correspondent, was transferred from the White House to Congress at the beginning of 1984. I asked her for her initial reaction as a journalist to Capitol Hill. "It's dangerous," she replied. By which she meant that there were too many spigots for turning on information. They could not all be covered at the same time, and so there were increased possibilities for missing a story. This is in contrast to the womb of the White House beat, where the mainstream journalist's basic assignment is to report on the daily activities of one person and the major competitive decision is only whether to lead with activity A

13. See Edwin R. Bayley, *Joe McCarthy and the Press* (Pantheon, 1981).
14. Douglass Cater, *The Fourth Branch of Government* (Vintage, 1959), p. 73.

or activity B. Suddenly it must have looked to Compton as if news could be gushing at the same time from Armed Services, Foreign Relations, Finance, and Budget. The notion in political science circles that diversity—all those publicity-seeking senators—is in the reporters' interests is only true in theory. Compton and her colleagues in the national media have to find ways to deal with the day's events in the time at hand. And it is here that the Senate's leaders become so important. They can be covered, just as the president can be covered: it is physically possible. And, of course, they are symbolically important. They are not just a senator from Tennessee or West Virginia; they are the majority or the minority, the Democrats or the Republicans, prolife or prochoice. Some months later, I again asked Compton for an assessment, and she did not again tell me that Congress was a dangerous place. It no longer was. She had learned the system.

By focusing so exclusively on the Senate leadership, our so-called ultimate insiders, the reporters are playing it safe. In their competitive and fast-moving world, they cover the Senate's agenda as guaranteed by the majority leader. These are journalists who pride themselves on understanding the arcane habits of the legislature. They graciously lead a stranger through the votes on a "perfecting amendment for the substitute amendment for the committee amendment." But only once in the year I was with them were they in front of events, namely when David Rogers of the *Wall Street Journal* broke the story that the Central Intelligence Agency was in charge of mining operations in the harbors of Nicaragua, which led to congressional action curbing U.S. participation.[15] A reporter looks around the Senate press gallery, at his friends at work, and says, "these are not hardball players."

The press covers what it covers because it thinks that what it covers is the most important. Today's Senate reporters would shake their heads in disbelief if told that the 1953 Senate reporters paid more attention to Wayne Morse than to Lyndon Johnson. It would be like equating the influence of Lowell Weicker and Bob Dole. Surely the maverick and the leader are not equally powerful

15. David Rogers, "U.S. Role in Mining Nicaraguan Harbors Reportedly Is Larger than First Thought," *Wall Street Journal*, April 6, 1984.

or even equally significant in the hindsight that is history. The 1980s reporters would be right. Washington journalists say that they are "serious" people; it is the highest accolade that they can bestow on themselves. "Serious" almost implies that reporters are willing to bore their audiences if they think a topic is worthy enough. This is especially important in an era that is dominated by budget debates. The 1983 national media ranking, which generally parallels the pecking order of the Senate, reflects a serious press corps, one that does not mean to be distracted by publicity stunts and unimportant players.

When the Republicans elected new Senate leaders at the end of 1984, Alan Simpson replaced Ted Stevens as the party's whip. A national media ranking for 1985 would undoubtedly show increased coverage of Simpson and decreased coverage of Stevens just as a 1985 rating would show Bob Dole, the new majority leader, as the ultimate insider. Dole, Simpson, and Stevens have not changed as individuals, of course, but their perceived quotient of power within the Senate has, and this is what the national press corps attempts to reflect in its reportage. Occasionally there is a consensus that a senator has power without having position, and he or she then rises in standing. This is usually the result of being accepted by fellow senators as having outstanding intellectual and conceptual ability. Robert A. Taft in the 1940s was an example of this rare phenomenon.[16] In the absence of precise measurements, however, reporters usually accept a major leadership post—chairman or ranking minority member of an "A" committee—as sufficient proof of insider status.

National reporters reduce the high drama of the Senate to manageable proportions (that is, a small enough cast of characters to be dealt with in 500–800 words or 90 seconds), while sorting out the players in terms of their roles. For example, there is always a part for the chairman of the Foreign Relations Committee. Since 1953 there have been eight chairmen, from Alexander Wiley to Richard Lugar, with very different styles, yet the only major difference from the media's perspective has been whether they are

16. See Roger H. Davidson, "Senate Leaders: Janitors for an Untidy Chamber?" in Lawrence C. Dodd and Bruce I. Oppenheimer, eds., *Congress Reconsidered*, 3d ed. (CQ Press, 1985), p. 227.

opponents or supporters of the president. The former get more attention.

Assigning roles becomes the how (the way the national media winnow the Senate from one hundred to twenty members) and why (the reason national coverage focuses on the ultimate insiders). The assortment of roles that is available for the national reporter to portray is illustrated in excerpts from a front-page lead story in the *New York Times* of March 21, 1984, by Martin Tolchin. Note particularly the role of leading opponent: it is always a good part for a senator who would not have been automatically noticed by the press in that it fits the mainstream media's tradition of balance (finding two sides to every story). Charles Mathias, who was a leading opponent in the Ninety-eighth Congress, told me that his phone often started ringing at 6:30 in the morning with "reporters asking for comments on things that I've never heard of. I say, 'Explain it to me and I'll comment.' "

AMENDMENT DRIVE ON SCHOOL PRAYER LOSES SENATE VOTE

The Republican-controlled Senate today rejected President Reagan's proposed constitutional amendment to permit organized spoken prayer in the public schools.
       the plot

the cast, in order of appearance

Senator Alfonse M. D'Amato, New York Republican, was the only metropolitan Senator to support the amendment.
    the local
(not for clients outside the New York area.)[17]

Senator Gary Hart, Colorado Democrat campaigning for his party's Presidential nomination, came back from the Illinois primary to vote against the amendment. . . .
    the potential presidential nominee

Senator Lowell P. Weicker, Jr., Connecticut Republican . . . concluded the two-week debate by asking, "Why forefeit our birthright of religious liberty for a mess of speculative, political pottage?"
    the leading opponent

17. The *New York Times* runs a supplemental news service that sells its major stories and columns to other news outlets.

Senator Howard H. Baker, Jr., of Tennessee . . . said the issue was "whether to restore the neutrality of the state in the free exercise of religion, or specifically reaffirm the antireligious bias of our schools."	*the majority leader*
"I blame the failure of this amendment on President Reagan's unwillingness to reach a compromise," said Senator Dennis DeConcini, Arizona Democrat.	*the surrogate minority leader*[18]
Senator Orrin G. Hatch, Utah Republican . . . praised the President's efforts and integrity.	*the committee chairman*
[Senator Jesse] Helms warned his colleagues after the vote that he would renew his efforts to restrict the jurisdiction of the Federal courts regarding school prayer, abortion and busing.	*the leading proponent*

Contrast this cast of characters with the story of the same day filed by Lee Bandy for the Columbia, South Carolina, *State*:

THURMOND, HOLLINGS DENOUNCE VOTE

Sen. Strom Thurmond, R-S.C., accused the Senate Tuesday of ignoring "the overwhelming majority of Americans who solidly favor a return of prayer in the public schools."

Expressing disappointment with the vote against a constitutional amendment to allow voluntary, spoken prayer in public schools, Thurmond vowed to press forward with efforts to restore prayers in the schools.

Sen. Ernest F. Hollings, D-S.C., who supported the amendment, blamed the Supreme Court for creating and nurturing "an antireligious bias in our schools. . . . "

Assorted senators—D'Amato, Hart, Weicker, Baker, DeConcini, Hatch, Helms—play parts in Tolchin's *New York Times* story. But Senators Thurmond and Hollings are Bandy's story, which was

18. Under most circumstances, this part would have played by the actual minority leader, Robert Byrd; on this issue, however, Byrd voted for the president's amendment, and a surrogate had to be anointed.

designed exclusively for South Carolina readers. The regional media cover senators; the national media cover the Senate. In the national media's story, the potential presidential nominee is a product of the election calendar (1984 in this case) and is chosen by forces outside the Senate. The leading proponent and opponent need not be committee chairmen and ranking minority members (if not, however, they are then anointed as temporary leaders); otherwise, the role-playing model of national media news determines that the emphasis always will be on the Senate's formal leadership structure. Treating senators as actors for whom there is a specific role to be played is just another way that reporters manage to tame the constant flow of material from which they must make their selections.[19]

It may be that national press coverage weakens the authority of congressional leaders by its characterization of them: How positive, how negative is the news? This is an empirical question outside the scope of this study. (My impression as a heavy news user, however, is that most congressional reportage is blandly neutral.)[20]

What we do know from this study is that the national press does not fragment power within Congress. It is not lured to the junior members as some have claimed. Neither good looks nor clever views can compete with the aphrodisia of a leadership position. So long as the Senate lives by seniority, Senator Blowdried will never be able to compete with Senator Mandarin for sustained attention on the network evening news or in large-circulation newspapers. The national press corps is not guilty as charged of being one of the decentralizing forces within Congress. On the contrary. It turns out to have a centripetal effect, moving news

19. For an excellent discussion of other ways that journalists choose their material, see Herbert J. Gans, *Deciding What's News* (Pantheon, 1979), pp. 78–115.

20. In a study of news about Congress that appeared in ten major newspapers during one month in 1978, two researchers concluded "that these papers tend toward neutrality and balance in their treatment of Congress . . . [but also] the press on the whole has little good to report about Congress and its membership." See Charles M. Tidmarch and John J. Pitney, Jr., "Covering Congress," *Polity*, vol. 17 (Spring 1985), pp. 480–81. Also see Arthur H. Miller, Edie N. Goldenberg, and Lutz Erbring, "Type-Set Politics: Impact of Newspapers on Public Confidence," *American Political Science Review*, vol. 73 (March 1979), pp. 67–84; and Michael J. Robinson and Kevin R. Appel "Network News Coverage of Congress," *Political Science Quarterly*, vol. 94 (Fall 1979), pp. 407–18.

away from the edges.[21] Moreover, despite the fears of Senate elders, televising the daily floor activities would continue to keep the locus of media attention on the Senate's leadership, judging from the way the networks have covered the House of Representatives, whose sessions have been televised since March 1979.[22]

Given the legitimate fears of scholars and others that today's patterns of congressional behavior pose "the risk that the institution will eventually disintegrate into atomized individualism,"[23] the national media's focus on the Senate's leadership and its disinterest in more marginal figures is both surprising and welcome. There have been times when the leaders of Congress were rightly accused of being too powerful; the present is otherwise, however. Thus any press attention that is in the interest of institutional stability is all to the good. That the national media is a positive force in correcting the ills Congress has created for itself is to claim too much. But if the national press is not part of the solution, at least this study shows it is not part of that problem. Of course there will come a time, as there always does in the cyclical history of congressional power, when the pendulum will swing away from the "diffusion of authority" that was discussed in chapter one. Reformers and others will then point an accusing finger at the reporters of the national media for unilaterally shrinking the one-hundred-member elected Senate by four-fifths—to a mere twenty senators deemed worthy of their attention—and they will ask, who elected you?

21. The growth of local radio and TV news coverage from Washington, on the other hand, does have centrifugal consequences, which is the subject of the next Newswork volume.

22. According to Foote and Weber, the top twenty members of the House of Representatives in terms of mentions on the networks' evening news in 1981–82 were Thomas P. O'Neill, Robert H. Michel, James Wright, Dan Rostenkowski, Phil Gramm, James Jones, Jack Kemp, Claude Pepper, Barber Conable, Henry Reuss, Joseph Addabbo, Delbert Latta, Silvio Conte, Millicent Fenwick, Leon Panetta, Morris Udall, Charles Stenholm, Paul McCloskey, Toby Moffett, and David Obey. Also, Timothy Cook shows that media coverage of the House leadership actually increased after floor proceedings were put on television; see "Newsmakers, Lawmakers and Leaders."

23. Steven S. Smith, "New Patterns of Decisionmaking in Congress," in Chubb and Peterson, eds. The New Direction in American Politics, pp. 219–20; also see Burdett A. Loomis, "The 'Me Decade' and the Changing Context of House Leadership," in Frank H. Mackaman, ed., Understanding Congressional Leadership (CQ Press, 1981), pp. 157–79.

VII

Influence, an Epilogue

"IN WASHINGTON TODAY," wrote William L. Rivers, a Stanford professor who used to be the Washington correspondent for a national
magazine, "correspondents who report for the news media pos-
sess a power beyond even their own dreams and fears."[1] "The
Imperial Media," columnist Joseph Kraft called them. "In the past
two decades," he wrote in 1981, "those of us in the press and
television have undergone a startling transformation. . . . We have
moved from the sidelines to a place at the center of the action."
Kraft made it clear that he was writing about "the relative handful
of national news enterprises—the three networks; the newsmagazines; and the one or two leading regional papers which most of us
read."[2] In his memoir Daniel Schorr illustrated the perceived
power of the media: "In the corridor of the Senate Office Building,
I ran into Senator Hubert Humphrey trying to round up a quorum
for a hearing of the Joint Congressional Economic Committee.
Half-jokingly, half-despairingly, he asked if I could install dummy
cameras and turn on some bright lights to attract truant members
of his committee."[3]

These authors are engaged in "public speak," of course. Washington journalists as a rule do not sit around telling each other

1. *The Other Government: Power and the Washington Media* (Universe, 1982), p. 10.
2. "The Imperial Media," *Commentary*, vol. 71 (May 1981), p. 36.
3. *Clearing the Air* (Houghton Mifflin, 1977), p. 287.

how influential or powerful (the words are used interchangeably) the national news media have become.[4] But there are also very few like James Reston of the *New York Times* who say, "our power is smaller than our reputation."[5]

There is no shortage of claims for the power of the press on Capitol Hill. Starting with the classic study by Donald Matthews in 1960, scholars and others seem to agree that "reporters play an important role in the operation of the Senate and profoundly shape the behavior of its members."[6] More recently, Joel Havemann of the *Los Angeles Times* wrote that "a complex but symbiotic relationship has developed between Congress and the news media. It is a relationship that begins in the self-interest of both, yet ultimately helps shape everything from next year's election returns to the most far-reaching of public policy decisions."[7] So many knowledgeable people, including senators, tell us that this is so that surely it must be so.[8]

The most obvious reason why influence is attributed to the media is that the members of Congress, and especially their staffs, are incorrigible news junkies. Michael J. Robinson and Maura E. Clancey have quantified this phenomenon. "The average senior [congressional] staff member claims to spend almost two and a half hours per day watching, reading or listening to these national news media," they wrote in *Washington Journalism Review*.[9] As I

4. On the other hand, two researchers claim that "the media's elite [has chosen] itself as preeminent in the race for influence." They base this assessment on a sample of journalists who were asked whether they should have more influence than the following groups: blacks, business, consumer groups, feminists, intellectuals, unions. It is a strange "race" that the researchers have constructed. While it sheds light on journalists' attitudes toward various groups, it does not ask whether journalists want to be powerful. See S. Robert Lichter and Stanley Rothman, "Media and Business Elites," *Public Opinion*, vol. 4 (October/November 1981), pp. 59–60.

5. *The Artillery of the Press* (Harper & Row, 1967), p. 71. Also see Anthony Smith, "The Influence of Television," *Daedalus*, vol. 114 (Fall 1985), pp. 1–15, although his skeptical assessment of the medium's impact is not specifically about television news.

6. U.S. *Senators & Their World* (Vintage, 1960), p. 203.

7. "Congress, Media: Odd Bedfellows," *Los Angeles Times*, October 29, 1983.

8. For example, see Richard Reeves, "Why Howard Baker Is Leaving the Senate," *Parade Magazine* (August 7, 1983), pp. 10–11.

9. "King of the Hill," *Washington Journalism Review*, vol. 5 (July/August 1983), p. 47.

wandered through Senator Moynihan's offices at 8:45 on a January morning, the scene reminded me of those cartoon ads for the old *Philadelphia Bulletin* ("nearly everyone in Philadelphia reads the *Bulletin*"): the senator's administrative assistant, personal secretary, press secretary, assistant press secretary, and office manager were all hidden behind a morning newspaper. Heavy consumption may not be bad for one's health, but it seems logical to assume that it will have an effect.

The problem is that cause and effect are so difficult to match up. One of the few times that the connection has been certain came in early 1977 when the *Washington Post*, the newspaper with the largest readership on Capitol Hill, assigned reporter T. R. Reid to follow week by week a little-known piece of legislation through Congress. The *Post*'s editors chose a perennial loser called the "waterway user charge bill" (it would require those who ship freight on the nation's canals and rivers to help the government pay for waterway maintenance). This time the bill passed. Its chief Senate sponsor, Pete Domenici, told Reid, "You know, there's probably 500 good policy ideas floating around on the Hill at any one time, but most of them just aren't getting on the front page of the *Post* every week."[10]

During the year I spent as an observer at the Senate, I did not see any cause and effect. I saw a lot of reporters writing stories. I saw a lot of bills being voted up or down. The stories often helped explain the votes, but I do not think the stories caused the votes. Yet it was a year in which the lawyer for the attorney general-designate accused Senator Howard Metzenbaum of "systematically leaking" material to the press that was "inflammatory" and "extremely prejudicial" to his client;[11] a year in which a private investigator admitted taping conversations in which a member of the Senate Labor Committee staff was leaking information to

10. *Congressional Odyssey: The Saga of a Senate Bill* (W. H. Freeman, 1980), p. 130. Another type of cause and effect case would be the Jack Anderson columns that led to the censure of Senator Thomas Dodd. See James Boyd, *Above the Law* (New American Library, 1968).

11. Mary Thornton, "Meese Failed to List Paid Trips," *Washington Post*, April 6, 1984, and "Attorneys for Meese Protest the Release of Travel Documents," *Washington Post*, April 7, 1984.

columnist Jack Anderson about the committee's investigation of the secretary of labor;[12] a year in which Senators Barry Goldwater and Daniel P. Moynihan jointly rebuked Senator Jesse Helms for disclosing information from the Senate Intelligence Committee, a charge that Helms vehemently denied.[13] Obviously there were interactions between senators (or their surrogates) and journalists that were intended to be (as Havemann puts it) "in the self-interest of both." Still, they caused remarkably few ripples that could be said to have nudged public policy questions in a manner that might not have happened had they not been reported in the national media. And so it is because my observations turn out to be counterintuitive that I choose to conclude this study with some thoughts on the influence of the national press on Capitol Hill.

Joseph Califano, who has watched Congress from an executive-branch perspective, has noted, "Look at the *Congressional Record* in the House on any significant debate and you can find 50 good quotes because they're all fighting to be one of those guys who gets into the [Dan] Rather coverage."[14] Since we now know that members of Congress hardly ever make the CBS evening news unless they are running for president or hold leadership positions, this could be described as a catalytic effect—the media changing the behavior of Congress without actually entering the process itself. The importance of the national media, then, would be not what it reports (and can be held accountable for), but simply that it is there; not what gets on the air or in print, but what members of Congress try to get on the air or in print. We should not discount the effect of the media just because we cannot measure it. (But neither should we accept its influence solely on the basis of intuitive reasoning.) In fact, in Califano's example what the members of the House are doing in the "50 good quotes" is primarily trying

12. George Lardner, Jr., "FBI Probes Investigation of Hill Staff Involved in Donovan Case," *Washington Post*, May 15, 1984, and "Data Came from Reporter, Ex-Prober Says," *Washington Post*, May 19, 1984.

13. Martin Tolchin, "Helms at Center of Controversy on Disclosures," *New York Times*, May 17, 1984, and "Senators Warned To Keep Secrets," *New York Times*, May 18, 1984.

14. Martin Linsky, *Impact: How the Press Affects Federal Policymaking* (Norton, forthcoming), chapter 4.

to get their local TV and radio stations to show them in action from the House floor. They are often successful, and Dan Rather does not have much to do with their behavior.

Because most senators (and House members) get almost no attention in the national media, it is not necessary for them to engage the national press corps in their legislative strategies. If they want to get a bill passed—to get from here to there in the legislative process—they rarely make the journey by mobilizing the press. Trying to use the media to get legislation through Congress is a Rube Goldberg design based on (A) legislator influencing (B) reporter to get information into (C) news outlet so as to convince (D) voters who will then put pressure on (E) other legislators. Given all of the problems inherent in successfully maneuvering through the maze, no wonder that legislative strategies are usually variations of (A) legislator asking (E) other legislators for their support through personal conversation, "Dear Colleague" letters, caucuses, or other means. Of course, some legislators, acting out of optimism or ignorance or arrogance, may choose to use the media even though it is a highly inefficient legislative strategy.

Occasionally I saw a senator call a press conference for what I felt was a pedagogical purpose, trying to educate reporters to the importance or intricacies of an issue. Generally, however, most of the press relations that I watched in 1984 involved the three activities that David Mayhew concluded are "electorally useful [for legislators] to engage in"—advertising, credit claiming, and position taking—that is, trying to create a favorable image with messages that have little content, showing that pleasing things happen because voters had the wisdom to elect a particular legislator, and making judgmental statements that are expected to agree with the views of certain constituencies.[15] Any handful of press releases from the rack in the Senate press gallery would be similar to these from the office of Senator Pete Wilson:

WILSON AVALANCHE BILL HAS SMOOTH SLEDDING THROUGH COMMITTEE (April 11, 1984)

15. David R. Mayhew, *Congress: The Electoral Connection* (Yale University Press, 1974), pp. 49, 52, 61–62.

WILSON TO SUPPORT FLEXIBLE WAGE RANGE FOR SUMMER JOBS
(May 17, 1984)

CALIFORNIA WATER PROJECTS GET BOOST FROM SENATOR WILSON
(May 24, 1984)

WILSON TO OFFER LEGISLATION TO BACK U.S. TUNA INDUSTRY
(June 25, 1984)

WILSON PRAISES NOMINATIONS TO CALIFORNIA COURT
(August 2, 1984)

While I was interviewing in the Senate, Timothy E. Cook was interviewing in the House of Representatives for a study to be called "The Ascent of the Congressional Press Secretary."[16] The forty press secretaries in his representative sample were "all but unanimous" that their purpose was "the care and feeding of the media in the home district." Only fifteen "made some spontaneous reference to the utility of the media in the legislative process." Cook in the House and I in the Senate agreed that reelection was the central goal of legislators' media strategies. There are exceptions. It is primarily a nonelective media strategy that Senator Proxmire pursues when he sends out a press release each month announcing the Golden Fleece Award for "the most wasteful, ridiculous, or ironic use of the taxpayers' money." (Of course, this also helps him with the voters of Wisconsin.) Nor should anyone ever underestimate the ego of a politician so that one is never quite sure whether publicity is not its own reward. But Dorothy Collin, a national reporter for the *Chicago Tribune*, said that the local reporters in the press corps are really the ones that their senators most carefully watch. Two desks away from Collin in the press gallery, Lee Bandy, who works for a newspaper in Columbia, South Carolina, had just written a Sunday column speculating on whether Governor Riley would challenge Senator Hollings in 1986.[17] "Don't you think the Hollings staff will be meeting on that

16. "Marketing the Members: The Ascent of the Congressional Press Secretary," paper delivered at the 1985 annual meeting of the Midwest Political Science Association.

17. "Will Riley go against Hollings?" Columbia (S.C.) *State*, July 29, 1984.

one?" National reporters, of course, may play the same role for the handful of senators who have immediate presidential aspirations. Still, most of what they write from Capitol Hill is much more straightforward in purpose: what you see is all there is (as opposed to the coverage of the White House and State Department, which often reflects "informed sources" who may have hidden agendas).

The Congress and the White House are at either end of Pennsylvania Avenue, but as news beats they are worlds apart. To say that one is open and the other is closed is to define just a part of the difference. Yet it is an important distinction, one that also contrasts the executive and legislative branches of the national government. With the exception of certain information that executive agencies give to the Foreign Relations, Armed Services, and Intelligence committees, the Senate of the United States really has no secrets.[18] (Which is not the same as saying that there are not some things that each senator would prefer not to share with journalists.) The part of executive government that I have elsewhere called "the Golden Triangle"—White House, State Department, Pentagon—resembles one big secret.[19] Most of what is discussed behind closed doors, whether military, diplomatic, or political, the participants want to keep to themselves. (Which is not the same as saying that national security would be endangered if some of the deliberations were revealed.) Those who are part of the executive branch have certain obligations to an organization; moreover, each agency has certain controls over its members. The organization's internal information takes on a privileged character, although, obviously, this is often breached.[20] But a legislative body consists of people who are only responsible for themselves and, in the absence of strong political parties, can only count on their

18. Very real questions were raised in 1984, however, about whether Congress could keep its national security secrets from the press. See Henry J. Hyde, "Can Congress Keep a Secret?" *National Review* (August 24, 1984), pp. 46, 61; Cord Meyer, "Hill Can't Stop Leaking?" *Washington Times*, May 25, 1984; and Jonathan Fuerbringer, "Joint Panel Urged for Intelligence," *New York Times*, August 1, 1984.

19. "The Golden Triangle: The Press at the White House, State, and Defense," *Brookings Review* (Summer 1983), pp. 14–19.

20. Stephen Hess, "Leaks and Other Informal Communications" *Society*, vol. 22 (January/February 1985), pp. 20–29.

own initiative to retain their positions. There are hardly any institutional checks on their behavior, including their relations with journalists. When Howard Baker was part of the committee investigating Watergate, he quipped, "The Ervin Committee did not invent the leak, but we elevated it to its highest art form."[21] The difference between the Ervin Committee members and other senators has nothing to do with individual morality; they simply possessed information that was more valuable as news.[22]

This attitude toward information, far more than the physical safety of presidents, determines access. (Although protective security measures have contributed to the closed world of the White House press corps.) Senators are so continuously available that the strange research design of this study was not to make appointments to interview them but simply to catch them for strolling conversations as we walked between their offices and the Senate chamber. (It proved to be a successful strategy, even when I approached them as a stranger; it would have been impossible in executive agencies, however.)

The twin facts that the legislature tends to be open and accessible and that the Golden Triangle tends to be a closed environment in which important information is given to journalists who are admitted by invitation makes a profound difference in the roles of the respective press corps and their importance (influence, power) in political Washington. The congressional reporters for national outlets—free to open doors, with sources everpresent—are far less important than the comparable and confined reporters of the White House and State Department beats. This is an irony that Washington journalists live with and is one of the reasons why reporters often rotate from the congressional beat (a happy assignment) to the White House beat (an unhappy assignment) but rarely make the professional move in the other direction.

The national media—notably the *New York Times* and the *Washington Post*—become major movers of information around the Golden Triangle, almost like journalist bumble bees spreading

21. James Hamilton, *The Power to Probe: A Study of Congressional Investigations* (Random House, 1976), p. 273.

22. Joseph Nocera, "The Art of the Leak," *Washington Monthly* (July/August 1979), p. 23.

pollen from White House to State Department to Pentagon to State to White House. Foreign embassies and others may also be players. Valuable information comes from a single source ("a high administration official said today . . . "). The source basically controls what is in the story. Others on the same wavelength think they know the identity of the source and the meaning of the message even if general readers do not. In this bizarre manner the national media gladly allow themselves to be participants in government, thus assuring that their reportage will be studied by the right people and that they will be the envy of lesser journalists.

This is not a congressional game. Martin Tolchin of the New York Times, who has covered both the White House and the Senate, notes, "There are no one-source stories on the Hill as in the executive. If a senator gives me a story I will then check with twelve people and it won't come out the way he wants it to." The story will be more complete but less important by the standards of influence that determine rank in the capital. In the pecking order that I developed in The Washington Reporters, the diplomatic beat (the most frequent site of insider stories) ranks first and the congressional beat is sixth.[23]

There is some signaling through the media by Senate leaders who wish to send messages to the White House. But they are so blatant, says the Post's Helen Dewar, that reporters know how to assess their intentions. In the year that I watched the majority leader's press secretary, Tommy Griscom, in his Capitol alcove briefings for the congressional press corps, he never resorted to the type of cuing that is a ritual at the White House and State Department, where "I can't confirm or deny" may mean "It's true, but I won't say that on the record." When Griscom was asked to assess the chances of Baker's pet project (a bill to televise the Senate proceedings), which we all knew was doomed to defeat, he replied, "Paul, don't ask. I haven't lied to you in four years, and I'm not going to start now."[24]

Also, it is not necessary for senators to use the press as an

23. The Washington Reporters (Brookings, 1981), p. 49.
24. For an interesting article on the role that Griscom played in the Ninety-seventh Congress, see Martin Tolchin, "A Press Secretary Can Say Things a Senator Can't," New York Times, April 20, 1983.

internal means of communication. Officials of the State Department and the Pentagon have remarkably few opportunities to interact with one another, but each reads what the other is thinking as reported in the pages of the *Washington Post* and *New York Times* (papers that are widely circulated throughout agencies by means of press clipping services).[25] Senators do not need reporters to speak for them because Capitol Hill is a very small enclave, physically and socially. During the fight over who would succeed Howard Baker as Republican leader, for example, I asked Bob Packwood if competing senators were using leaks and columns like "Washington Whispers" [in U.S. *News & World Report*]. He replied, "That would be a dangerous game. There are only fifty-four of us." (In fact, one contender for the leadership post later appeared in "Washington Whispers" in what had all the signs of a press secretary's plant. The senator was badly defeated, although again there is no way of knowing whether the story contributed to the outcome.)

There is an impression, especially from viewing television, that the national media favor the presidency over Congress. As political scientist Doris A. Graber has written, "the presidency is a single-headed body, readily personified, filmed, and recorded in the visible person of the chief executive. . . . By contrast, Congress is a many-headed hydra with no single widely familiar personal focus."[26] Commenting on what is apparently an institutional bias, Senator Leahy told me, "It's not surprising. You see the same thing in the states, where the governors overshadow the legislators." The consequences of this sustained and sharply focused media attention on the president have been the subject of recent debate. Based on the experiences of Jimmy Carter, Lloyd N. Cutler (his counsel in 1979–80) explained how White House aides live with the "recurring sense of a TV doomsday clock" because a "president and his advisers feel bound to make a response [to an ominous story on television news] in time for the next evening news broadcast." Cutler concludes, "The most harmful effect of TV news is its tendency to speed up the decisionmaking process

25. See Stephen Hess, *The Government/Press Connection: Press Officers and Their Offices* (Brookings, 1984), pp. 41–45.

26. *Mass Media and American Politics* (CQ Press, 1980), p. 209.

on issues that TV news is featuring and to slow down and interrupt the process of deciding other important issues that get less TV attention. . . . In a very real sense, TV lead stories now set the priorities for the policymaking agenda."[27] Yet based on his experience covering the first term of Ronald Reagan's presidency, Steven R. Weisman of the *New York Times* reports that the next president after Carter "achieved a new level of control over the mechanics of modern communication. . . . Central to the President's overall strategy has been his unusual ability to deal with television and print reporters on his own terms—to decide when, where and how he will engage them. In short, the art of controlled access."[28] But whether the media manipulate the president or the president manipulates the media, this relationship and its critics have invested the national media with an aura of influence that is totally inappropriate, in my opinion, in comparable discussions of Congress and the press. On the basis of a questionnaire completed by congressional leaders and high executive appointees in recent administrations, Martin Linsky of Harvard's School of Government will conclude in a forthcoming book that "members of Congress are less worried about negative press than are the bureaucrats [executive agency personnel]. They see it as going with the territory and understand the element of truth in the cliché about yesterday's articles being today's fish wrapping."[29]

The notion that journalists impose upon Congress their view of what is significant—as some scholars contend—is not the impression I brought back from my observations.[30] What Congress is doing at any one time is determined by many factors not directly influenced by the press—the inflation rate, the unemployment

27. Lloyd N. Cutler, "Foreign Policy on Deadline," *Foreign Policy,* no. 56 (Fall 1984), pp. 114, 121.

28. "The President and the Press," *New York Times Magazine* (October 14, 1984), p. 34.

29. *Impact: How the Press Affects Federal Policymaking,* chapter 6. Also note the good-humored comment of former Senator Edmund Muskie: "Looking at yourself through the media is like looking at one of those rippled mirrors in an amusement park. You recognize yourself—but it doesn't look like the image you see in your morning mirror." John Nielsen and Fred Coleman, "The Muskie Manner," *Newsweek* (May 26, 1980), p. 45.

30. See Susan H. Miller, "News Coverage of Congress: the Search for the Ultimate Spokesman," *Journalism Quarterly,* vol. 54 (Autumn 1977), p. 465.

rate, the crime rate, what the president asks the Congress to do, controversial decisions of the Supreme Court, acts of terrorists, acts of nature. The order of business is set by the majority leader, the ultimate insider, after consultation with his committee chairmen.[31] What is then reported in the national media is largely a reflection of this process. The popular judgment of journalism researchers that "the press does not tell the people what to think, it tells the people what to think about" is simply not the case on Capitol Hill.[32] This press corps is almost totally reactive.

National reporters also may become less influential on Capitol Hill as additional sources of information become available to the legislators and their assistants. Writing about the role of the press in the Israeli legislature, for instance, Dorit Phyllis Gary concludes, "since Knesset members do not enjoy large staffs, most of the legislative queries and motions are based on media reports. . . ."[33] But U.S. senators and members of the House of Representatives now have very large staffs, and they produce for their employers a type of tailor-made material that suits specific legislative and political needs.[34] One step removed from the research designed for legislators' personal needs are the large committee staffs that service their party needs and ideological needs. Various sorts of computerized services, just now coming to the Senate, will give staffs even more information that is not depen-

31. For useful discussions of the role of the party leaders in the Senate, see Roger H. Davidson, "Senate Leaders: Janitors for an Untidy Chamber?" in Lawrence C. Dodd and Bruce I. Oppenheimer, eds., *Congress Reconsidered*, 3d ed. (CQ Press, 1985), pp. 225–52; and Robert L. Peabody, "Senate Party Leadership: From the 1950s to the 1980s," in Frank H. Mackaman, ed., *Understanding Congressional Leadership* (CQ Press, 1981), pp. 51–115.

32. See Bernard C. Cohen, *The Press and Foreign Policy* (Princeton University Press, 1965), p. 13.

33. "Letter from Israel," *Columbia Journalism Review*, vol. 23 (November/December 1984), p. 48. Comparing the United States and the United Kingdom, Lionel Barber, a reporter for London's *Financial Times* who spent a summer at the *Washington Post*, wrote, "A whole army of aides, staffers, and researchers support Congress, while some members of Parliament can afford only a single secretary-cum-typist. In my experience, the British journalist is often better informed about pending policy moves in the government than the British MP. . . ." See "Covering the U.S.A.," *presstime* (November 1985), pp. 38–39.

34. For the most current information on the growth of congressional staffs, see Norman J. Ornstein and others, eds., *Vital Statistics on Congress, 1984–1985 Edition* (American Enterprise Institute, 1984), chapter 5.

dent on the news media.[35] While the local media provide vital information about state or district affairs, events covered in the national media are rarely actionable, even though they may be important and interesting.[36] Legislators listening to the network news are mostly like the rest of us, shaking our heads over the sad state of affairs in Chad or Centralia.

There are, however, certain specialized publications that retain their influence because they are precise enough to help legislators and their assistants in their work. A member of the Senate Finance Committee staff, for example, might subscribe to *Daily Tax Report* or *Tax Notes*, a weekly magazine. Probably every office relies on *Congressional Quarterly*. Sitting at a table reserved for the press in a Capitol dining room in August 1984, Dale Tale of *Congressional Quarterly* told me, "Most stories [by other reporters] today will say, 'The Senate is tied up in procedural knots,' and then move on. But I will have to write a story about the procedural knots."

Ultimately, a lot more people and groups have an interest in noting the power of the press than in showing that media power sometimes may be akin to that of the Wizard of Oz. There is, of course, the press itself. As Hedley Donovan, the former editor in chief of *Time*, observed with regard to President Kennedy, "We loved being read so closely."[37] There are also certain participants in the governmental process who must find it useful to blame "media power" for their own failures or frustrations.[38] Books about the power that is will always sell better than those about the

35. For the increased use of computers on Capitol Hill, see Stephen Frantzich, "Communications and Congress," in Gerald Benjamin, ed., *The Communication Revolution in Politics*, Proceedings of the Academy of Political Science, vol. 34 (1982), pp. 91–96; Michael J. Robinson, "Three Faces of Congressional Media," pp. 59–62; Steve Blakely, "Computers Alter Way Congress Does Business," *Congressional Quarterly Weekly Report*, vol. 43 (July 13, 1985), pp. 1379–82; and Tim Miller, "Stan Parris' Little Black Book Has 400,000 Names in It," *Washington Post Magazine* (June 23, 1985), pp. 12–14.

36. Greg Schneiders also argues that the networks' evening news programs have been cutting back on their coverage of Congress. See "The 90-Second Handicap: Why TV Coverage of Legislation Falls Short," *Washington Journalism Review*, vol. 7 (June 1985), p. 44; also see Norman Ornstein and Michael Robinson, "The Case of Our Disappearing Congress," *TV Guide* (January 11, 1986), pp. 4–10.

37. *Roosevelt to Reagan* (Harper & Row, 1985), p. 74.

38. The most obvious example is the speech that then Vice-President Spiro Agnew gave in Des Moines, Iowa, on November 13, 1969, in which he attacked the

power that is not. And finally, there are media researchers whose entitlements in the world of conference going and journal articles—regardless of whether we are praising, pointing with alarm, or remaining truly neutral—will be in direct proportion to our colleagues' sense that we are writing about one of the real power players in public policy. This then becomes a collective bias of which readers should be aware. Beware.

---

television networks as "a concentration of power over American public opinion unknown in history." A week later, speaking before the Montgomery, Alabama, Chamber of Commerce, Agnew expanded his criticism of the media to include the power of the *New York Times* and *Washington Post*. See Francis and Ludmila Voelker, eds., *Mass Media: Forces in Our Society* (Harcourt Brace Jovanovich, 1972), pp. 263–70.

Appendix A

Senate Leadership Positions, 1983

Andrews, Mark (R-N.Dak.)	Chairman, Select Committee on Indian Affairs
Baker, Howard H., Jr. (R-Tenn.)	Majority leader
Bentsen, Lloyd (D-Tex.)	Chairman, Democratic Senatorial Campaign Committee
Biden, Joseph R., Jr. (D-Del.)	Ranking Democrat, Judiciary Committee
Byrd, Robert C. (D-W.Va.)	Minority leader
Chiles, Lawton (D-Fla.)	Ranking Democrat, Budget Committee
Cranston, Alan (D-Calif.)	Minority whip; and ranking Democrat, Veterans' Affairs Committee
Dole, Robert J. (R-Kans.)	Chairman, Finance Committee
Domenici, Pete V. (R-N.Mex.)	Chairman, Budget Committee
Eagleton, Thomas F. (D-Mo.)	Ranking Democrat, Governmental Affairs Committee
Ford, Wendell H. (D-Ky.)	Ranking Democrat, Rules and Administration Committee

Garn, Edwin J. (Jake) (R-Utah) — Chairman, Banking, Housing, and Urban Affairs Committee

Goldwater, Barry (R-Ariz.) — Chairman, Select Committee on Intelligence

Hatch, Orrin G. (R-Utah) — Chairman, Labor and Human Resources Committee

Hatfield, Mark O. (R-Oreg.) — Chairman, Appropriations Committee

Heinz, John (R-Pa.) — Chairman, Select Committee on Aging

Helms, Jesse A. (R-N.C.) — Chairman, Agriculture, Nutrition, and Forestry Committee

Hollings, Ernest F. (D-S.C.) — Ranking Democrat, Commerce, Science and Transportation Committee

Huddleston, Walter D. (D-Ky.) — Ranking Democrat, Agriculture, Nutrition, and Forestry Committee

Inouye, Daniel K. (D-Hawaii) — Secretary, Democratic Conference

Jackson, Henry M. (D-Wash.) — Ranking Democrat, Armed Services Committee

Jepsen, Roger W. (R-Iowa) — Chairman, Joint Economic Committee

Johnston, J. Bennett (D-La.) — Ranking Democrat, Energy and Natural Resources Committee

Kennedy, Edward M. (D-Mass.) — Ranking Democrat, Labor and Human Resources Committee

Laxalt, Paul (R-Nev.) — General chairman, Republican National Committee

Long, Russell B. (D-La.) — Ranking Democrat, Finance Committee

Lugar, Richard G. (R-Ind.) — Chairman, National Republican Senatorial Committee

McClure, James A. (R-Idaho) — Chairman, Energy and Natural Resources Committee; and chairman, Republican Conference Committee

Mathias, Charles McC., Jr. (R-Md.) — Chairman, Rules and Administration Committee

Moynihan, Daniel Patrick (D-N.Y.) — Vice-chairman, Select Committee on Intelligence

Nunn, Sam (D-Ga.) — Ranking Democrat, Small Business Committee

Packwood, Bob (R-Oreg.) — Chairman, Commerce, Science, and Transportation Committee

Pell, Claiborne (D-R.I.) — Ranking Democrat, Foreign Relations Committee

Percy, Charles H. (R-Ill.) — Chairman, Foreign Relations Committee

Proxmire, William (D-Wis.) — Ranking Democrat, Banking, Housing, and Urban Affairs Committee

Randolph, Jennings (D-W.Va.) — Ranking Democrat, Environment and Public Works Committee

Roth, William V., Jr. (R-Del.) — Chairman, Governmental Affairs Committee

Simpson, Alan K. (R-Wyo.) — Chairman, Veterans' Affairs Committee

Stafford, Robert T. (R-Vt.) — Chairman, Environment and Public Works Committee

Stennis, John C. (D-Miss.) — Ranking Democrat, Appropriations Committee

Stevens, Ted (R-Alaska) — Majority whip; and chairman, Select Committee on Ethics

Thurmond, Strom (R-S.C.) — Chairman, Judiciary Committee; and president pro tempore of the Senate

Tower, John G. (R-Tex.) — Chairman, Armed Services Committee; and chairman, Republican Policy Committee

Weicker, Lowell P., Jr. (R-Conn.) — Chairman, Small Business Committee

Appendix B

Media Rankings of Senators, 1953–83

FOLLOWING ARE the years and sources for the media rankings of Senators that appear in tables B-1 through B-12.

1953–54	Associated Press
1964	Associated Press
1965–66	Associated Press
1965–66	*Time, Newsweek, U.S. News & World Report*
1965–66	*Reader's Guide to Periodical Literature; Time, Newsweek, U.S. News & World Report; Chicago Tribune, Des Moines Register, Kansas City Star, Los Angeles Times, Milwaukee Journal, St. Louis Post-Dispatch, Washington Post, Christian Science Monitor, New York Times, Louisville Courier-Journal.*
1969–70	Associated Press
1970–71	*Reader's Guide to Periodical Literature*

1973–74   Associated Press

1973–74   *Reader's Guide to Periodical Literature; Washington Post,*
            New Orleans Times-Picayune, Chicago Tribune, Los
            Angeles Times; ABC, CBS, NBC evening news.

1981–82   ABC, CBS, NBC evening news.

1982–84   50 TV programs, including "Nightline," "Good
            Morning America," "Today," "CBS Morning
            News," "20/20," "60 Minutes," "MacNeil/Lehrer
            Newshour," "C-Span Call-In," and "Take 2"
            (CNN).

1983   ABC, CBS, NBC evening news; "Meet the Press,"
            "Face the Nation," "This Week with David
            Brinkley"; *Christian Science Monitor, Los Angeles Times,*
            New York Times, Wall Street Journal, Washington Post.

Table B-1. *Number of Times Senators Were Mentioned in Associated Press Stories, 1953-54*

Senator	Times mentioned	Senator	Times mentioned
McCarthy, J. (R-Wis.)	358	Johnston, O. (D-S.C.)	49
Knowland, W. (R-Calif.)	226	Jenner, W. (R-Ind.)	48
Morse, W. (I-Oreg.)	175	Monroney, A. (D-Okla.)	47
Kefauver, E. (D-Tenn.)	126	Cordon, G. (R-Oreg.)	46
Humphrey, H. (D-Minn.)	116	Johnson, E. (D-Colo.)	46
Johnson, L. (D-Tex.)	113	Hendrickson, R. (R-N.J.)	45
Langer, W. (R-N.Dak.)	113	Neely, M. (D-W.Va.)	44
Ferguson, H. (R-Mich.)	108	Young, M. (R-N.Dak.)	44
Capehart, H. (R-Ind.)	102	McClellan, J. (D-Ark.)	43
Anderson, C. (D-N.Mex.)	98	Ellender, A. (D-La.)	42
Bricker, J. (R-Ohio)	95	Jackson, H. (D-Wash.)	41
Douglas, P. (D-Ill.)	95	Kerr, R. (D-Okla.)	41
Ives, I. (R-N.Y.)	84	Eastland, J. (D-Miss.)	39
Lehman, H. (D-N.Y.)	83	Fulbright, J. (D-Ark.)	39
Cooper, J. (R-Ky.)	77	Williams, J. (R-Del.)	39
Byrd, H., Sr. (D-Va.)	74	Kuchel, T. (R-Calif.)	37
Sparkman, J. (D-Ala.)	71	Magnuson, W. (D-Wash.)	36
Saltonstall, L. (R-Mass.)	67	Hickenlooper, B. (R-Iowa)	34
Gore, A., Sr. (D-Tenn.)	61	Chavez, D. (D-N.Mex.)	33
Hennings, T. (D-Mo.)	61	Hill, L. (D-Ala.)	33
Smith, H. (R-N.J.)	60	Barrett, F. (R-Wyo.)	32
Smith, M. (R-Maine)	60	Holland, S. (D-Fla.)	32
Aiken, G. (R-Vt.)	59	Long, R. (D-La.)	32
George, W. (D-Ga.)	58	Green, T. (D-R.I.)	31
Wiley, A. (R-Wis.)	57	Potter, C. (R-Mich.)	31
Dirksen, E. (R-Ill.)	54	Symington, S. (D-Mo.)	31
Russell, R. (D-Ga.)	54	Carlson, F. (R-Kans.)	29
Mundt, K. (R-S.Dak.)	51	Gillette, G. (D-Iowa)	29
Millikin, E. (R-Colo.)	50	Case, F. (R-S.Dak.)	28
Murray, J. (D-Mont.)	50	Kilgore, H. (D-W.Va.)	28

Table B-1 *(continued)*

Senator	Times mentioned	Senator	Times mentioned
Butler, J. (R-Md.)	27	Robertson, A. (D-Va.)	18
Kennedy, J. (D-Mass.)	27	Thye, E. (R-Minn.)	17
Schoeppel, A. (R-Kans.)	27	Mansfield, M. (D-Mont.)	15
Dworshak, H. (R-Idaho)	26	Duff, J. (R-Pa.)	14
Flanders, R. (R-Vt.)	26	Payne, F. (R-Maine)	13
Frear, J. (D-Del.)	25	Purtell, W. (R-Conn.)	13
Goldwater, B. (R-Ariz.)	25	Bennett, W. (R-Utah)	12
Watkins, A. (R-Utah)	24	Bush, P. (R-Conn.)	12
Clements, E. (D-Ky.)	23	Stennis, J. (D-Miss.)	12
Hayden, C. (D-Ariz.)	23	Martin, E. (R-Pa.)	8
Malone, G. (R-Nev.)	22	Beall, J., Sr. (R-Md.)	6
Daniel, P. (D-Tex.)	21		
Welker, H. (R-Idaho)	21		
Pastore, J. (D-R.I.)	20		
Smathers, G. (D-Fla.)	20		

Source: David H. Weaver and G. Cleveland Wilhoit, "News Media Coverage of U.S. Senators in Four Congresses, 1953-1974," *Journalism Monographs*, no. 67 (April 1980), pp. 12-13.

Table B-2. *Number of Times Senators Were Mentioned in Associated Press Stories*, 1964 (40 *days*)

Senator	Times mentioned	Senator	Times mentioned
Goldwater, B. (R-Ariz.)	223	Dodd, T. (D-Conn.)	4
Humphrey, H. (D-Minn.)	63	Hartke, V. (D-Ind.)	4
Dirksen, E. (R-Ill.)	41	Hill, L. (D-Ala.)	4
Keating, K. (R-N.Y.)	32	Johnston, O. (D-S.C.)	4
Mansfield, M. (D-Mont.)	31	McCarthy, E. (D-Minn.)	4
Thurmond, S. (R-S.C.)	20	McGovern, G. (D-S.Dak.)	4
Young, S. (D-Ohio)	19	Salinger, P. (D-Calif.)	4
Kennedy, E. (D-Mass.)	16	Talmadge, H. (D-Ga.)	4
Smith, M. (R-Maine)	15	Yarborough, R. (D-Tex.)	4
Scott, H. (R-Pa.)	13	Brewster, D. (D-Md.)	3
Javits, J. (R-N.Y.)	13	Clark, J. (D-Pa.)	3
Morse, W. (D-Oreg.)	9	Hayden, C. (D-Ariz.)	3
Morton, T. (R-Ky.)	9	Hruska, R. (R-Nebr.)	3
Fulbright, J. (D-Ark.)	8	McGee, G. (D-Wyo.)	3
Bayh, B. (D-Ind.)	8	Mechem, E. (R-N.Mex.)	3
Curtis, C. (R-Nebr.)	8	Monroney, A. (D-Okla.)	3
Jordan, B. (D-N.C.)	8	Mundt, K. (R-S.Dak.)	3
Williams, J. (R-Del.)	7	Muskie, E. (D-Maine)	3
Anderson, C. (D-N.Mex.)	6	Ribicoff, A. (D-Conn.)	3
Engle, C. (D-Calif.)	6	Robertson, A. (D-Va.)	3
Holland, S. (D-Fla.)	6	Tower, J. (R-Tex.)	3
Kuchel, T. (R-Calif.)	6	Aiken, G. (R-Vt.)	2
Long, R. (D-La.)	6	Allott, G. (R-Colo.)	2
Proxmire, W. (D-Wis.)	6	Bartlett, E. (D-Alaska)	2
Cooper, J. (R-Ky.)	5	Beall, J., Sr. (R-Md.)	2
Douglas, P. (D-Ill.)	5	Byrd, H., Sr. (D-Va.)	2
Hickenlooper, B. (R-Iowa)	5	Carlson, F. (R-Kans.)	2
Russell, R. (D-Ga.)	5	Case, C. (R-N.J.)	2
Smathers, G. (D-Fla.)	5	Cotton, N. (R-N.H.)	2
Cannon, H. (D-Nev.)	4	Eastland, J. (D-Miss.)	2

Table B-2 (*continued*)

Senator	Times mentioned	Senator	Times mentioned
Edmundson, J. (D-Okla.)	2	Saltonstall, L. (R-Mass.)	1
Ellender, A. (D-La.)	2	Stennis, J. (D-Miss.)	1
Ervin, S. (D-N.C.)	2	Symington, S. (D-Mo.)	1
Gore, A., Sr. (D-Tenn.)	2	Williams, H. (D-N.J.)	1
Jackson, H. (D-Wash.)	2	Bennett, W. (R-Utah)	0
McIntyre, T. (D-N.H.)	2	Bible, A. (D-Nev.)	0
Magnuson, W. (D-Wash.)	2	Boggs, J. (R-Del.)	0
Nelson, G. (D-Wis.)	2	Burdick, Q. (D-N.Dak.)	0
Neuberger, M. (D-Oreg.)	2	Byrd, R. (D-W.Va.)	0
Pastore, J. (D-R.I.)	2	Church, F. (D-Idaho)	0
Prouty, W. (R-Vt.)	2	Dominick, P. (R-Colo.)	0
Randolph, J. (D-W.Va.)	2	Inouye, D. (D-Hawaii)	0
Simpson, M. (R-Wyo.)	2	Jordan, L. (R-Idaho)	0
Sparkman, J. (D-Ala.)	2	Long, E. (D-Mo.)	0
Fong, H. (R-Hawaii)	1	McNamara, P. (D-Mich.)	0
Gruening, E. (D-Alaska)	1	Miller, J. (R-Iowa)	0
Hart, P. (D-Mich.)	1	Moss, F. (D-Utah)	0
Lausche, F. (D-Ohio)	1	Pell, C. (D-R.I.)	0
McClellan, J. (D-Ark.)	1	Pearson, J. (R-Kans.)	0
Metcalf, L. (D-Mont.)	1	Walters, H. (D-Tenn.)	0
		Young, M. (R-N.Dak.)	0

Source: G. Cleveland Wilhoit and Kenneth S. Sherrill, "Wire Service Visibility of U.S. Senators," *Journalism Quarterly*, vol. 45 (Spring 1968), p. 45.

Table B-3. *Number of Times Senators Were Mentioned in Associated Press Stories, 1965-66*

Senator	Times mentioned	Senator	Times mentioned
Dirksen, E. (R-Ill.)	217	Tydings, J. (D-Md.)	31
Kennedy, R. (D-N.Y.)	209	McClellan, J. (D-Ark.)	29
Mansfield, M. (D-Mont.)	121	Metcalf, L. (D-Mont.)	29
Javits, J. (R-N.Y.)	120	Mondale, W. (D-Minn.)	29
Douglas, P. (D-Ill.)	87	Monroney, A. (D-Okla.)	29
Dodd, T. (D-Conn.)	67	Yarborough, R. (D-Tex.)	28
Kennedy, E. (D-Mass.)	66	Pearson, J. (R-Kans.)	28
Tower, J. (R-Tex.)	57	Miller, J. (R-Iowa)	28
Fulbright, J. (D-Ark.)	57	Ribicoff, A. (D-Conn.)	27
Morse, W. (D-Oreg.)	56	Smith, M. (R-Maine)	26
Long, R. (D-La.)	54	Proxmire, W. (D-Wis.)	26
Cooper, J. (R-Ky.)	54	Harris, F. (D-Okla.)	26
Williams, J. (R-Del.)	51	Hickenlooper, B. (R-Iowa)	25
Saltonstall, L. (R-Mass.)	47	Randolph, J. (D-W.Va.)	25
Morton, T. (R-Ky.)	47	Hart, P. (D-Mich.)	24
Scott, H. (R-Pa.)	45	Bennett, W. (R-Utah)	24
Clark, J. (D-Pa.)	45	Hruska, R. (R-Nebr.)	23
Thurmond, S. (R-S.C.)	43	Lausche, F. (D-Ohio)	22
Stennis, J. (D-Miss.)	43	Murphy, G. (R-Calif.)	22
Curtis, C. (R-Nebr.)	42	Neuberger, M. (D-Oreg.)	22
Russell, R. (D-Ga.)	39	Pastore, J. (D-R.I.)	21
McCarthy, E. (D-Minn.)	39	Pell, C. (D-R.I.)	21
Bayh, B. (D-Ind.)	39	Aiken, G. (R-Vt.)	21
Kuchel, T. (R-Calif.)	38	Bass, R. (D-Tenn.)	21
Jordan, B. (D-N.C.)	38	Ervin, S. (D-N.C.)	21
Case, C. (R-N.J.)	38	Jordan, L. (R-Idaho)	20
Eastland, J. (D-Miss.)	36	Gore, A., Sr. (D-Tenn.)	18
Sparkman, J. (D-Ala.)	34	Hartke, V. (D-Ind.)	17
Ellender, A. (D-La.)	32	Hayden, C. (D-Ariz.)	17
Mundt, K. (R-S.Dak.)	31	Boggs, J. (D-Del.)	17

Table B-3 (*continued*)

Senator	Times mentioned	Senator	Times mentioned
Muskie, E. (D-Maine)	17	Long, E. (D-Mo.)	9
Symington, S. (D-Mo.)	16	Burdick, Q. (D-N.Dak.)	8
Allott, G. (R-Colo.)	16	Carlson, F. (R-Kans.)	8
McIntyre, T. (D-N.H.)	15	Fong, H. (R-Hawaii)	8
Dominick, P. (R-Colo.)	14	Moss, F. (D-Utah)	8
Holland, S. (D-Fla.)	14	Nelson, G. (D-Wis.)	8
Prouty, W. (R-Vt.)	14	Williams, H. (D-N.J.)	7
Smathers, G. (D-Fla.)	14	McGee, G. (D-Wyo.)	7
Simpson, M. (R-Wyo.)	13	Cannon, H. (D-Nev.)	7
Fannin, P. (R-Ariz.)	13	Bible, A. (D-Nev.)	5
Jackson, H. (D-Wash.)	13	Gruening, E. (D-Alaska)	5
Bartlett, E. (D-Alaska)	12	Inouye, D. (D-Hawaii)	5
Church, F. (D-Idaho)	12	McGovern, G. (D-S.Dak.)	5
Talmadge, H. (D-Ga.)	12	Montoya, J. (D-N.Mex.)	5
Young, S. (D-Ohio)	11	Byrd, R. (D-W.Va.)	3
Magnuson, W. (D-Wash.)	11		
Brewster, D. (D-Md.)	11		
Cotton, N. (R-N.H.)	10		
Young, M. (R-N.Dak.)	10		
Hill, L. (D-Ala.)	9		

Source: David H. Weaver and G. Cleveland Wilhoit, "News Media Coverage of U.S. Senators in Four Congresses, 1953-1974," *Journalism Monographs*, no. 67 (April 1980), pp. 16–17.

Table B-4. *Number of Times Senators Were Mentioned in Three Newsmagazines, 1965-66 (24 issues of each)*

Senator	Times mentioned	Senator	Times mentioned
Kennedy, R. (D-N.Y.)	136	Sparkman, J. (D-Ala.)	9
Dirksen, E. (R-Ill.)	71	Church, F. (D-Idaho)	8
Mansfield, M. (D-Mont.)	57	Clark, J. (D-Pa.)	8
Fulbright, J. (D-Ark.)	53	Curtis, C. (R-Nebr.)	8
Kennedy, E. (D-Mass.)	42	Ellender, A. (D-La.)	8
Javits, J. (R-N.Y.)	36	Hayden, C. (D-Ariz.)	8
Douglas, P. (D-Ill.)	26	Magnuson, W. (D-Wash.)	8
Morse, W. (D-Oreg.)	26	McCarthy, E. (D-Minn.)	8
Russell, R. (D-Ga.)	24	McGovern, G. (D-S.Dak.)	8
Ribicoff, A. (D-Conn.)	23	McIntyre, T. (D-N.H.)	8
Stennis, J. (D-Miss.)	23	Miller, J. (R-Iowa)	8
Tower, J. (R-Tex.)	19	Mundt, K. (R-S.Dak.)	8
Dodd, T. (D-Conn.)	17	Neuberger, M. (D-Oreg.)	8
McClellan, J. (D-Ark.)	17	Pell, C. (D-R.I.)	8
Long, R. (D-La.)	14	Thurmond, S. (R-S.C.)	8
Aiken, G. (R-Vt.)	13	Bennett, W. (R-Utah)	7
Case, C. (R-N.J.)	12	Ervin, S. (D-N.C.)	7
Eastland, J. (D-Miss.)	12	Hickenlooper, B. (R-Iowa)	7
Saltonstall, L. (R-Mass.)	12	Robertson, A. (D-Va.)	7
Williams, J. (R-Del.)	12	Smathers, G. (D-Fla.)	7
Cooper, J. (R-Ky.)	11	Young, S. (D-Ohio)	7
Gruening, E. (D-Alaska)	11	Boggs, J. (R-Del.)	6
Nelson, G. (D-Wis.)	11	Byrd, R. (D-W.Va.)	6
Metcalf, L. (D-Mont.)	10	Hart, P. (D-Mich.)	6
Murphy, G. (R-Calif.)	10	McGee, G. (D-Wyo.)	6
Hartke, V. (D-Ind.)	9	Morton, T. (R-Ky.)	6
Jackson, H. (D-Wash.)	9	Randolph, J. (D-W.Va.)	6
Kuchel, T. (R-Calif.)	9	Talmadge, H. (D-Ga.)	6
Lausche, F. (D-Ohio)	9	Tydings, J. (D-Md.)	6
Smith, M. (R-Maine)	9	Bartlett, E. (D-Alaska)	5

Table B-4 (continued)

Senator	Times mentioned	Senator	Times mentioned
Fong, H. (R-Hawaii)	5	Allott, G. (R-Colo.)	3
Gore, A., Sr. (D-Tenn.)	5	Bayh, B. (D-Ind.)	3
Hill, L. (D-Ala.)	5	Cannon, H. (D-Nev.)	3
Monroney, A. (D-Okla.)	5	Carlson, F. (R-Kans.)	3
Proxmire, W. (D-Wis.)	5	Dominick, P. (R-Colo.)	3
Scott, H. (R-Pa.)	5	Fannin, P. (R-Ariz.)	3
Symington, S. (D-Mo.)	5	Harris, F. (D-Okla.)	3
Anderson, C. (D-N.Mex.)	4	Holland, S. (D-Fla.)	3
Bass, R. (D-Tenn.)	4	Jordan, L. (R-Idaho)	3
Brewster, D. (D-Md.)	4	Yarborough, R. (D-Tex.)	3
Burdick, Q. (D-N.Dak.)	4	Young, M. (R-N.Dak.)	3
Inouye, D. (D-Hawaii)	4	Bible, A. (D-Nev.)	2
Jordan, B. (D-N.C.)	4	Cotton, N. (R-N.H.)	2
Long, E. (D-Mo.)	4	Hruska, R. (R-Nebr.)	2
Mondale, W. (D-Minn.)	4	Montoya, J. (D-N.Mex)	2
Moss, F. (D-Utah)	4	Muskie, E. (D-Maine)	2
Pastore, J. (D-R.I.)	4	Williams, H. (D-N.J.)	2
Pearson, J. (R-Kans.)	4		
Prouty, W. (R-Vt.)	4		
Simpson, M. (R-Wyo.)	4		

Source: David H. Weaver and G. Cleveland Wilhoit, "News Magazine Visibility of Senators," *Journalism Quarterly*, vol. 51 (Spring 1974), p. 69.

Table B-5. *Number of Times Senators Appeared in Media Indexes,*
1965-66

Senator	Times appearing	Senator	Times appearing
Kennedy, R. (D-N.Y.)	708	Clark, J. (D-Pa.)	68
Dirksen, E. (R-Ill.)	566	Cooper, J. (R-Ky.)	67
Mansfield, M. (D-Mont.)	420	Ervin, S. (D-N.C.)	67
Fulbright, J. (D-Ark.)	301	Thurmond, S. (R-S.C.)	67
Javits, J. (R-N.Y.)	280	Gruening, E. (D-Alaska)	60
Kennedy, E. (D-Mass.)	233	Hartke, V. (D-Ind.)	60
Morse, W. (D-Oreg.)	227	Morton, T. (R-Ky.)	60
Dodd, T. (D-Conn.)	171	Church, F. (D-Idaho)	59
Douglas, P. (D-Ill.)	142	Magnuson, W. (D-Wash.)	57
Long, R. (D-La.)	120	McGovern, G. (D-S.Dak.)	57
Kuchel, T. (R-Calif.)	116	Neuberger, M. (D-Oreg.)	55
McClellan, J. (D-Ark.)	100	Pell, C. (D-R.I.)	55
Russell, R. (D-Ga.)	93	Lausche, F. (D-Ohio)	54
Miller, J. (R-Iowa)	91	Saltonstall, L. (R-Mass.)	54
Long, E. (D-Mo.)	90	Tower, J. (R-Tex.)	54
Hart, P. (D-Mich.)	84	Monroney, A. (D-Okla.)	53
Aiken, G. (R-Vt.)	83	Brewster, D. (D-Md.)	50
Bayh, B. (D-Ind.)	83	Curtis, C. (R-Nebr.)	48
Murphy, G. (R-Calif.)	83	Anderson, C. (D-N.Mex.)	45
Stennis, J. (D-Miss.)	81	McCarthy, E. (D-Minn.)	45
Tydings, J. (D-Md.)	80	Byrd, R. (D-W.Va.)	43
Case, C. (R-N.J.)	79	Prouty, W. (R-Vt.)	43
Eastland, J. (D-Miss.)	79	Sparkman, J. (D-Ala.)	43
Scott, H. (R-Pa.)	79	Carlson, F. (R-Kans.)	42
Ribicoff, A. (D-Conn.)	78	Fong, H. (R-Hawaii)	40
Proxmire, W. (D-Wis.)	76	Bible, A. (D-Nev.)	39
Williams, J. (R-Del.)	75	Hruska, R. (R-Nebr.)	39
Nelson, G. (D-Wis.)	72	Dominick, P. (R-Colo.)	37
Hickenlooper, B. (R-Iowa)	70	Randolph, J. (D-W.Va.)	37
Symington, S. (D-Mo.)	70	Yarborough, R. (D-Tex.)	37

Table B-5 (continued)

Senator	Times appearing	Senator	Times appearing
Young, S. (D-Ohio)	37	Talmadge, H. (D-Ga.)	27
Ellender, A. (D-La.)	36	Bass, R. (D-Tenn.)	26
Hayden, C. (D-Ariz.)	36	Bennett, W. (R-Utah)	25
Metcalf, L. (D-Mont.)	36	Boggs, J. (R-Del.)	25
Pastore, J. (D-R.I.)	35	Holland, S. (D-Fla.)	25
Jordan, B. (D-N.C.)	34	Burdick, Q. (D-N.Dak.)	24
Mundt, K. (R-S.Dak.)	34	Hill, L. (D-Ala.)	22
Pearson, J. (R-Kans.)	34	McIntyre, T. (D-N.H.)	22
Gore, A., Sr. (D-Tenn.)	33	Young, M. (R-N.Dak.)	22
Jackson, H. (D-Wash.)	33	Cannon, H. (D-Nev.)	21
McGee, G. (D-Wyo.)	33	Jordan, L. (R-Idaho)	21
Smith, M. (R-Maine)	33	Fannin, P. (R-Ariz.)	20
Smathers, G. (D-Fla.)	31	Harris, F. (D-Okla.)	19
Williams, H. (D-N.J.)	31	Allott, G. (R-Colo.)	18
Muskie, E. (D-Maine)	30	Cotton, N. (R-N.H.)	18
Bartlett, E. (D-Alaska)	29	Montoya, J. (D-N.Mex.)	13
Mondale, W. (D-Minn.)	28		
Inouye, D. (D-Hawaii)	27		
Moss, F. (D-Utah)	27		
Simpson, M. (R-Wyo.)	27		

Source: David H. Weaver and others, "Senatorial News Coverage: Agenda-Setting for Mass and Elite Media in the United States," in *Senate Communications with the Public*, prepared for the Commission on the Operation of the Senate, 94th Cong. 2 sess. (Government Printing Office, 1977), pp. 50-52. The survey included senators mentioned in 250 popular magazines indexed in the *Reader's Guide to Periodical Literature*, 1965-66; 24 issues each from *Time*, *Newsweek*, and U.S. *News & World Report*, 1965-66; 56 days each (224 issues) of the *Washington Post*, *Christian Science Monitor*, *New York Times*, and *Louisville Courier-Journal*, 1965; and 56 days each (336 issues) of the *Chicago Tribune*, *Des Moines Register*, *Kansas City Star*, *Los Angeles Times*, and *Milwaukee Journal*, 1965.

Table B-6. *Number of Times Senators Were Mentioned in Associated Press Stories, 1969-70*

Senator	Times mentioned	Senator	Times mentioned
Mansfield, M. (D-Mont.)	335	Byrd, R. (D-W.Va.)	70
Kennedy, E. (D-Mass.)	330	Jackson, H. (D-Wash.)	70
Scott, H. (R-Pa.)	269	Percy, C. (R-Ill.)	70
McGovern, G. (D-S.Dak.)	209	Cook, M. (R-Ky.)	66
Muskie, E. (D-Maine)	198	Hartke, V. (D-Ind.)	66
Goodell, C. (R-N.Y.)	185	Moss, F. (D-Utah)	66
Fulbright, J. (D-Ark.)	183	Aiken, G. (R-Vt.)	65
Bayh, B. (D-Ind.)	172	Allott, G. (R-Colo.)	64
Griffin, R. (R-Mich.)	140	Hughes, H. (D-Iowa)	61
Hart, P. (D-Mich.)	135	Mondale, W. (D-Minn.)	61
Harris, F. (D-Okla.)	131	Williams, H. (D-N.J.)	58
McCarthy, E. (D-Minn.)	130	Cranston, A. (D-Calif.)	53
Tydings, J. (D-Md.)	123	Holland, S. (D-Fla.)	53
Proxmire, W. (D-Wis.)	122	Tower, J. (R-Tex.)	53
Javits, J. (R-N.Y.)	120	Baker, H. (R-Tenn.)	52
Hruska, R. (R-Nebr.)	118	Russell R. (D-Ga.)	52
Cooper, J. (R-Ky.)	117	Nelson, G. (D-Wis.)	51
Ervin, S. (D-N.C.)	105	McGee, G. (D-Wyo.)	50
Eastland, J. (D-Miss.)	102	Pastore, J. (D-R.I.)	49
Goldwater, B. (R-Ariz.)	99	Young, S. (D-Ohio)	49
Thurmond, S. (R-S.C.)	96	Burdick, Q. (D-N.Dak.)	47
Stennis, J. (D-Miss.)	95	Byrd, H., Jr. (D-Va.)	46
Long, R. (D-La.)	91	Case, C. (R-N.J.)	46
Church, F. (D-Idaho)	89	Symington, S. (D-Mo.)	46
Gore, A., Sr. (D-Tenn.)	89	Fong, H. (R-Hawaii)	45
Hatfield, M. (R-Oreg.)	89	Fannin, P. (R-Ariz.)	43
Dole, R. (R-Kans.)	82	Mathias, C. (R-Md.)	43
Dodd, T. (D-Conn.)	81	Prouty, W. (R-Vt.)	43
Brooke, E. (R-Mass.)	78	McClellan, J. (D-Ark.)	42
Yarborough, R. (D-Tex.)	78	Ribicoff, A. (D-Conn.)	42

Table B-6 (*continued*)

Senator	Times mentioned	Senator	Times mentioned
Montoya, J. (D-N.Mex.)	41	Pell, C. (D-R.I.)	25
Bennett, W. (R-Utah)	40	Eagleton, T. (D-Mo.)	24
Saxbe, W. (R-Ohio)	40	Randolph, J. (D-W.Va.)	24
Smith, M. (R-Maine)	39	Stevens, T. (R-Alaska)	24
Ellender, A. (D-La.)	38	Anderson, C. (D-N.Mex.)	22
Schweiker, R. (R-Pa.)	38	Gravel, M. (D-Alaska)	21
Gurney, E. (R-Fla.)	38	Metcalf, L. (D-Mont.)	21
Hollings, E. (D-S.C.)	37	Spong, W. (D-Va.)	21
Magnuson, W. (D-Wash.)	36	Jordan, L. (R-Idaho)	20
Curtis, C. (R-Nebr.)	33	Miller, J. (R-Iowa)	20
Allen, J. (D-Ala.)	32	Bible, A. (D-Nev.)	19
Cannon, H. (D-Nev.)	31	Talmadge, H. (D-Ga.)	19
Dominick, P. (R-Colo.)	31	Hansen, C. (R-Wyo.)	18
Pearson, J. (R-Kans.)	30	Boggs, J. (R-Del.)	16
Mundt, K. (R-S.Dak.)	28	Bellmon, H. (R-Okla.)	15
Inouye, D. (D-Hawaii)	27	Young, M. (R-N.Dak.)	14
Packwood, B. (R-Oreg.)	27	Jordan, B. (D-N.C.)	10
Cotton, N. (R-N.H.)	26		
McIntyre, T. (D-N.H.)	26		
Sparkman, J. (D-Ala.)	26		

Source: David H. Weaver and G. Cleveland Wilhoit, "News Media Coverage of U.S. Senators in Four Congresses, 1953-1974," *Journalism Monographs*, no. 67 (April 1980), pp. 20-21.

Table B-7. *Number of Times Senators Appeared in* Reader's Guide to Periodical Literature, 1970-71

Senator	Times mentioned	Senator	Times mentioned
Kennedy, E. (D-Mass.)	133	Ervin, S. (D-N.C.)	4
Muskie, E. (D-Maine)	40	Hughes, H. (D-Iowa)	4
McCarthy, E. (D-Minn.)	36	Russell, R. (D-Ga.)	4
Fulbright, J. (D-Ark.)	27	Yarborough, R. (D-Tex.)	4
Goodell, C. (R-N.Y.)	24	Byrd, H., Jr. (D-Va.)	3
Goldwater, B. (R-Ariz.)	14	Cooper, J. (R-Ky.)	3
Stennis, J. (D-Miss.,)	13	Dodd, T. (D-Conn.)	3
McGovern, G. (D-S.Dak.)	11	Hart, P. (D-Mich.)	3
Mansfield, M. (D-Mont.)	11	Hollings, E. (D-S.C.)	3
Ribicoff, A. (D-Conn.)	11	Long, R. (D-La.)	3
McClellan, J. (D-Ark.)	10	Magnuson, W. (D-Wash.)	3
Proxmire, W. (D-Wis.)	10	Moss, F. (D-Utah)	3
Harris, F. (D-Okla.)	9	Pell, C. (D-R.I.)	3
Nelson, G. (D-Wis.)	9	Allott, G. (R-Colo.)	2
Church, F. (D-Idaho)	8	Baker, H. (R-Tenn.)	2
Jackson, H. (D-Wash.)	8	Bible, A. (D-Nev.)	2
Pastore, J. (D-R.I.)	8	Byrd, R. (D-W.Va.)	2
Scott, H. (R-Pa.)	8	Hansen, C. (R-Wyo.)	2
Tydings, J. (D-Md.)	8	Hruska, R. (R-Nebr.)	2
Gore, A., Sr. (D-Tenn.)	7	Metcalf, L. (D-Mont.)	2
Javits, J. (R-N.Y.)	7	Packwood, B. (R-Oreg.)	2
Smith, M. (R-Maine)	7	Percy, C. (R-Ill.)	2
Symington, S. (D-Mo.)	7	Williams, H. (D-N.J.)	2
Brooke, E. (R-Mass.)	5	Allen, J. (D-Ala.)	1
Cranston, A. (D-Calif.)	5	Bennett, W. (R-Utah)	1
Hatfield, M. (R-Oreg.)	5	Case, C. (R-N.J.)	1
Mondale, W. (D-Minn.)	5	Cook, M. (R-Ky.)	1
Thurmond, S. (R-S.C.)	5	Curtis, C. (R-Nebr.)	1
Bayh, B. (D-Ind.)	4	Eagleton, T. (D-Mo.)	1
Dole, R. (R-Kans.)	4	Eastland, J. (D-Miss.)	1

Table B-7 (*continued*)

Senator	Times mentioned	Senator	Times mentioned
Ellender, A. (D-La.)	1	Cannon, H. (D-Nev.)	0
Fannin, P. (R-Ariz.)	1	Cotton, N. (R-N.H.)	0
Griffin, R. (R-Mich.)	1	Dominick, P. (R-Colo.)	0
Hartke, V. (D-Ind.)	1	Fong, H. (R-Hawaii)	0
McGee, G. (D-Wyo.)	1	Gravel, M. (D-Alaska)	0
McIntyre, T. (D-N.H.)	1	Gurney, E. (R-Fla.)	0
Mathias, C. (R-Md.)	1	Holland, S. (D-Fla.)	0
Miller, J. (R-Iowa)	1	Inouye, D. (D-Hawaii)	0
Pearson, J. (R-Kans.)	1	Jordan, B. (D-N.C.)	0
Prouty, W. (R-Vt.)	1	Jordan, L. (R-Idaho)	0
Randolph J. (D-W.Va.)	1	Montoya, J. (D-N.Mex.)	0
Saxbe, W. (R-Ohio)	1	Mundt, K. (R-S.Dak.)	0
Spong, W. (D-Va.)	1	Schweiker, R. (R-Pa.)	0
Tower, J. (R-Tex.)	1	Sparkman, J. (D-Ala.)	0
Young, S. (D-Ohio)	1	Stevens, T. (R-Alaska)	0
Aiken, G. (R-Vt.)	0	Talmadge, H. (D-Ga.)	0
Anderson, C. (D-N.Mex.)	0	Young, M. (R-N.Dak.)	0
Bellmon, H. (R-Okla.)	0		
Boggs, J. (R-Del.)	0		
Burdick, Q. (D-N.Dak.)	0		

Source: David H. Weaver and others, "Senatorial News Coverage: Agenda-Setting for Mass and Elite Media in the United States," in *Senate Communications with the Public*, prepared for the Commission on the Operation of the Senate, 94th Cong. 2 sess. (Government Printing Office, 1977), pp. 53-55.

Table B-8. *Number of Times Senators Were Mentioned in Associated Press Stories,* 1973-74

Senator	Times mentioned	Senator	Times mentioned
Kennedy, E. (D-Mass.)	212	Brooke, E. (R-Mass.)	42
Mansfield, M. (D-Mont.)	203	Symington, S. (D-Mo.)	41
Jackson, H. (D-Wash.)	169	Tunney, J. (D-Calif.)	39
McGovern, G. (D-S.Dak.)	153	Mathias, C. (R-Md.)	39
Scott, H. (R-Pa.)	132	Case, C. (R-N.J.)	39
Humphrey, H. (D-Minn.)	121	Hartke, V. (D-Ind.)	36
Muskie, E. (D-Maine)	108	Williams, H. (D-N.J.)	35
Ervin, S. (D-N.C.)	106	Cranston, A. (D-Calif.)	35
Proxmire, W. (D-Wis.)	103	Buckley, J. (R-N.Y.)	35
Javits, J. (R-N.Y.)	101	Hruska, R. (R-Nebr.)	34
Fulbright, J. (D-Ark.)	91	Nelson, G. (D-Wis.)	34
Byrd, R. (D-W.Va.)	84	Hart, P. (D-Mich.)	33
Mondale, W. (D-Minn.)	79	Sparkman, J. (D-Ala.)	32
Percy, C. (R-Ill.)	73	Ribicoff, A. (D-Conn.)	32
Tower, J. (R-Tex.)	70	Helms, J. (R-N.C.)	31
Church, F. (D-Idaho)	69	Cotton, N. (R-N.H.)	31
Goldwater, B. (R-Ariz.)	68	Cook, M. (R-Ky.)	31
Eagleton, T. (D-Mo.)	64	Pell, C. (D-R.I.)	31
Griffin, R. (R-Mich.)	60	Eastland, J. (D-Miss.)	31
Long, R. (D-La.)	56	Dominick, P. (R-Colo.)	30
Stennis, J. (D-Miss.)	53	Brock, B. (R-Tenn.)	30
Cannon, H. (D-Nev.)	52	Talmadge, H. (D-Ga.)	30
Bayh, B. (D-Ind.)	50	Weicker, L. (R-Conn.)	29
Hughes, H. (D-Iowa)	50	Abourezk, J. (D-S.Dak.)	28
Dole, R. (R-Kans.)	48	Gravel, M. (D-Alaska)	28
McClellan, J. (D-Ark.)	44	Hatfield, M. (R-Oreg.)	28
Allen, J. (D-Ala.)	44	Stevenson, A. (D-Ill.)	28
Bentsen, L. (D-Tex.)	44	Byrd, H., Jr. (I-Va.)	27
Baker, H. (R-Tenn.)	43	McGee, G. (D-Wyo.)	26
Magnuson, W. (D-Wash.)	43	Schweiker, R. (R-Pa.)	26

Table B-8 (*continued*)

Senator	Times mentioned	Senator	Times mentioned
Pastore, J. (D-R.I.)	25	McIntyre, T. (D-N.H.)	14
Bellmon, H. (R-Okla.)	25	Stevens, T. (R-Alaska)	14
Aiken, G. (R-Vt.)	23	Randolph, J. (D-W.Va.)	13
Thurmond, S. (R-S.C.)	23	Hansen, C. (R-Wyo.)	12
Bartlett, D. (R-Okla.)	22	Hathaway, W. (D-Maine)	12
Bennett, W. (R-Utah)	22	Inouye, D. (D-Hawaii)	12
Curtis, C. (R-Nebr.)	22	Chiles, L. (D-Fla.)	10
Moss, F. (D-Utah)	22	Fong, H. (R-Hawaii)	10
Scott, W. (R-Va.)	22	Metcalf, L. (D-Mont.)	10
Young, M. (R-N.Dak.)	22	Haskell, F. (D-Colo.)	9
Clark, D. (D-Iowa)	21	Johnston, J. (D-La.)	9
Biden, J. (D-Del.)	19	Bible, A. (D-Nev.)	8
Gurney, E. (R-Fla.)	19	Nunn, S. (D-Ga.)	8
Hollings, E. (D-S.C.)	19	Domenici, P. (R-N.Mex.)	7
Taft, R. Jr. (R-Ohio)	19	Stafford, R. (R-Vt.)	7
Fannin, P. (R-Ariz.)	18	Montoya, J. (D-N.Mex.)	7
Beall, J., Jr. (R-Md.)	16	Pearson, J. (R-Kans.)	6
Roth, W. (R-Del.)	16	Huddleston, W. (D-Ky.)	5
Packwood, B. (R-Oreg.)	15	Burdick, Q. (D-N.Dak.)	4
McClure, J. (R-Idaho)	15		

Source: David H. Weaver and G. Cleveland Wilhoit, "News Media Coverage of U.S. Senators in Four Congresses, 1953-1974," *Journalism Monographs*, no. 67 (April 1980), pp. 23-24.

Table B-9. *Number of Times Senators Appeared in Media Indexes,*
1973-74

Senator	Times mentioned	Senator	Times mentioned
Ervin, S. (D-N.C.)	1,967	Williams, H. (D-N.J.)	316
Jackson, H. (D-Wash.)	1,957	Talmadge, H. (D-Ga.)	314
Kennedy, E. (D-Mass.)	1,751	Hart, P. (D-Mich.)	304
Mansfield, M. (D-Mont.)	1,245	Bentsen, L. (D-Tex.)	281
McGovern, G. (D-S.Dak.)	1,093	Dole, R. (R-Kans.)	280
Javits, J. (R-N.Y.)	1,080	Symington, S. (D-Mo.)	277
Humphrey, H. (D-Minn.)	974	Hughes, H. (D-Iowa)	275
Proxmire, W. (D-Wis.)	874	Inouye, D. (D-Hawaii)	273
Scott, H. (R-Pa.)	853	Case, C. (R-N.J.)	268
Percy, C. (R-Ill.)	844	Hartke, V. (D-Ind.)	267
Baker, H. (R-Tenn.)	836	Griffin, R. (R-Mich.)	257
Muskie, E. (D-Maine)	806	Brooke, E. (R-Mass.)	252
Fulbright, J. (D-Ark.)	756	Eastland, J. (D-Miss.)	246
Goldwater, B. (R-Ariz.)	723	Magnuson, W. (D-Wash.)	240
Weicker, L. (R-Conn.)	720	Cannon, H. (D-Nev.)	232
Mondale, W. (D-Minn.)	610	Nelson, G. (D-Wis.)	226
Buckley, J. (R-N.Y.)	523	Pell, C. (D-R.I.)	215
Long, R. (D-La.)	512	McClellan, J. (D-Ark.)	209
Stennis, J. (D-Miss.)	504	Abourezk, J. (D-S.Dak.)	196
Byrd, R. (D-W.Va.)	500	Cook, M. (R-Ky.)	190
Stevenson, A. (D-Ill.)	489	Montoya, J. (D-N.Mex.)	184
Gurney, E. (R-Fla.)	461	Hatfield, M. (R-Oreg.)	182
Cranston, A. (D-Calif.)	447	Allen, J. (D-Ala.)	179
Tunney, J. (D-Calif.)	427	Moss, F. (D-Utah)	178
Bayh, B. (D-Ind.)	368	Sparkman, J. (D-Ala.)	167
Ribicoff, A. (D-Conn.)	342	Brock, B. (R-Tenn.)	163
Church, F. (D-Idaho)	340	Aiken, G. (R-Vt.)	156
Eagleton, T. (D-Mo.)	329	Schweiker, R. (R-Pa.)	153
Mathias, C. (R-Md.)	327	McGee, G. (D-Wyo.)	151
Tower, J. (R-Tex.)	318	Pastore, J. (D-R.I.)	146

Table B-9 *(continued)*

Senator	Times mentioned	Senator	Times mentioned
Dominick, P. (R-Colo.)	143	Stevens, T. (R-Alaska)	74
Scott, W. (R-Va.)	135	Bartlett, D. (R-Okla.)	73
Thurmond, S. (R-S.C.)	133	Hollings, E. (D-S.C.)	73
McIntyre, T. (D-N.H.)	128	Chiles, L. (D-Fla.)	62
Helms, J. (R-N.C.)	123	Metcalf, L. (D-Mont.)	62
Hruska, R. (R-Nebr.)	122	Bible, A. (D-Nev.)	61
Curtis, C. (R-Nebr.)	121	Biden, J. (D-Del.)	59
Gravel, M. (D-Alaska)	118	Pearson, J. (R-Kans.)	58
Beall, J., Jr. (R-Md.)	116	Hansen, C. (R-Wyo.)	57
Byrd, H., Jr. (I-Va.)	116	Hathaway, W. (D-Maine)	56
Bellmon, H. (R-Okla.)	111	Fong, H. (R-Hawaii)	54
Taft, R. Jr. (R-Ohio)	111	McClure, J. (R-Idaho)	49
Packwood, B. (R-Oreg.)	108	Haskell, F. (D-Colo.)	41
Clark, D. (D-Iowa)	102	Domenici, P. (R-N.Mex.)	39
Cotton, N. (R-N.H.)	101	Huddleston, W. (D-Ky.)	39
Young, M. (R-N.Dak.)	101	Nunn, S. (D-Ga.)	37
Johnston, J. (D-La.)	100	Roth, W. (R-Del.)	34
Bennett, W. (R-Utah)	97	Burdick, Q. (D-N.Dak.)	22
Randolph, J. (D-W.Va.)	92	Stafford, R. (R-Vt.)	17
Fannin, P. (R-Ariz.)	76		

Source: David H. Weaver and others, "Senatorial News Coverage: Agenda-Setting for Mass and Elite Media in the United States," in *Senate Communications with the Public*, prepared for the Commission on the Operation of the Senate, 94th Cong. 2 sess. (Government Printing Office, 1977), pp. 56-58. Survey covers 250 popular magazines included in the *Reader's Guide to Periodical Literature*; the *Washington Post, New Orleans Times-Picayune, Chicago Tribune*, and *Los Angeles Times* as listed in the *National Newspaper Index*; and the ABC, CBS, NBC evening news programs as listed in the *Television News Index* of Vanderbilt University.

Table B-10. *Number of Times Senators Were Mentioned on Network Television Evening News Programs, 1981-82*

Senator	Times mentioned	Senator	Times mentioned
Baker, H. (R-Tenn.)	360	Proxmire, W. (D-Wis.)	32
Kennedy, E. (D-Mass.)	197	Biden, J. (D-Del.)	31
Dole, R. (R-Kans.)	161	Leahy, P. (D-Vt.)	31
Byrd, R. (D-W.Va.)	113	Armstrong, W. (R-Colo.)	28
Helms, J. (R-N.C.)	107	Riegle, D. (D-Mich.)	28
Percy, C. (R-Ill.)	106	Long, R. (D-La.)	27
Cranston, A. (D-Calif.)	104	Dodd, C. (D-Conn.)	26
Domenici, P. (R-N.Mex.)	74	Quayle, D. (R-Ind.)	26
Glenn, J. (D-Ohio)	74	Lugar, R. (R-Ind.)	25
Hatch, O. (R-Utah)	73	Cannon, H. (D-Nev.)	24
Goldwater, B. (R-Ariz.)	66	Stevens, T. (R-Alaska)	24
Jackson H. (D-Wash.)	66	Sarbanes, P. (D-Md.)	23
Williams, H. (D-N.J.)	66	Denton, J. (R-Ala.)	22
Laxalt, P. (R-Nev.)	59	Bradley, B. (D-N.J.)	21
Packwood, B. (R-Oreg.)	57	Roth, W. (R-Del.)	21
Moynihan, D. (D-N.Y.)	57	Grassley, C. (R-Iowa)	20
Tower, J. (R-Tex.)	56	Johnston, J. (D-La.)	20
Hollings, E. (D-S.C.)	50	Kassebaum, N. (R-Kans.)	19
Hart, G. (D-Colo.)	49	Simpson, A. (R-Wyo.)	19
Hatfield, M. (R-Oreg.)	48	Stennis, J. (D-Miss.)	19
Tsongas, P. (D-Mass.)	48	Warner, J. (R-Va.)	19
Metzenbaum, H. (D-Ohio)	46	Andrews, M. (R-N.Dak.)	18
Thurmond, S. (R-S.C.)	41	Boschwitz, R. (R-Minn.)	18
Hayakawa, S. (R-Calif.)	38	Garn, J. (R-Utah)	18
Pell, C. (D-R.I.)	38	Heflin, H. (D-Ala.)	18
Pressler, L. (R-S.Dak.)	38	Heinz, J. (R-Pa.)	18
East, J. (R-N.C.)	37	Wallop, M. (R-Wyo.)	18
Weicker, L. (R-Conn.)	35	Bumpers, D. (D-Ark.)	17
Danforth, J. (R-Mo.)	34	Mathias C. (R-Md.)	17
Nunn, S. (D-Ga.)	32	Chafee, J. (R-R.I.)	17

Table B-10 (*continued*)

Senator	Times mentioned	Senator	Times mentioned
Schmitt, H. (R-N.Mex.)	16	Stafford, R. (R-Vt.)	7
DeConcini, D. (D-Ariz.)	13	Baucus, M. (D-Mont.)	6
Levin, C. (D-Mich.)	13	Humphrey, G. (R-N.H.)	6
Jepsen, R. (R-Iowa)	13	Cohen, W. (R-Maine)	6
Exon, J. (D-Nebr.)	13	Huddleston, W. (D-Ky.)	6
Durenburger, D. (R-Minn.)	12	Mattingly, M. (R-Ga.)	6
Sasser, J. (D-Tenn.)	12	Eagleton, T. (D-Mo.)	6
Zorinsky, E. (D-Nebr.)	11	D'Amato, A. (R-N.Y.)	6
Inouye, D. (D-Hawaii)	10	Byrd, H., Jr. (I-Va.)	6
Hawkins, P. (R-Fla.)	10	Rudman, W. (R-N.H.)	5
Pryor, D. (D-Ark.)	10	Bentsen, L. (D-Tex.)	5
Chiles, L. (D-Fla.)	9	Mitchell, G. (D-Maine)	4
Kasten, R. (R-Wis.)	9	Ford, W. (D-Ky.)	4
Randolph, J. (D-W.Va.)	9	Dixon, A. (D-Ill.)	4
Symms, S. (R-Idaho)	9	Nickles, D. (R-Okla.)	3
Specter, A. (R-Pa.)	8	Cochran, T. (R-Miss.)	3
McClure, J. (R-Idaho)	8	Murkowski, F. (R-Alaska)	2
Boren, D. (D-Okla.)	8	Abdnor, J. (R-S.Dak.)	2
Gorton, S. (R-Wash.)	8	Burdick, Q. (D-N.Dak.)	1
Melcher, J. (D-Mont.)	7	Matsunaga, S. (D-Hawaii)	1

Source: Adapted from Joe S. Foote and David J. Weber, "Network Evening News Visibility of Congressmen and Senators," paper prepared for the 1984 annual meeting of the Association for Education in Journalism and Mass Communication.

Table B-11. *Number of Times Senators Appeared on National Television other than on Network Evening News Programs, 1983-84 (268 days)*

Senator	Appearances	Senator	Appearances
Dole, R. (R-Kans.)	27	Simpson, A. (R-Wyo.)	3
Hollings, E. (D-S.C.)	18	Bradley, B. (D-N.J.)	3
Hart, G. (D-Colo.)	15	Bentsen, L. (D-Tex.)	3
Dodd, C. (D-Conn.)	14	Gorton, S. (R-Wash.)	3
Hatch, O. (R-Utah)	14	Cohen, W. (R-Maine)	3
Cranston, A. (D-Calif.)	12	Symms, S. (R-Idaho)	3
Glenn, J. (D-Ohio)	12	Kennedy, E. (D-Mass.)	2
Baker, H. (R-Tenn.)	10	Percy, C. (R-Ill.)	2
Tsongas, P. (D-Mass.)	10	Goldwater, B. (R-Ariz.)	2
Lugar, R. (R-Ind.)	8	Bumpers, D. (D-Ark.)	2
Specter, A. (R-Pa.)	8	D'Amato, A. (R-N.Y.)	2
Pressler, L. (R-S.Dak.)	7	Chiles, L. (D-Fla.)	2
Metzenbaum, H. (D-Ohio)	6	Roth, W. (R-Del.)	2
Nunn, S. (D-Ga.)	6	Long, R. (D-La.)	2
Kassebaum, N. (R-Kans.)	6	Thurmond, S. (R-S.C.)	2
Tower, J. (R-Tex.)	6	Leahy, P. (D-Vt.)	2
Moynihan, D. (D-N.Y.)	6	Exon, J. (D-Nebr.)	2
Laxalt, P. (R-Nev.)	5	Nickles, D. (R-Okla.)	2
Stevens, T. (R-Alaska)	5	Sarbanes, P. (D-Md.)	2
Weicker, L. (R-Conn.)	5	Jackson, H. (D-Wash.)	1
Armstrong, W. (R-Colo.)	5	Byrd, R. (D-W.Va.)	1
East, J. (R.-N.C.)	5	Kasten, R. (R-Wis.)	1
Biden, J. (D-Del.)	4	Packwood, B. (R-Oreg.)	1
Proxmire, W. (D-Wis.)	4	Wilson, P. (R-Calif.)	1
Denton, J. (R-Ala.)	4	Hatfield, M. (R-Oreg.)	1
Levin, C. (D-Mich.)	4	Garn, J. (R-Utah)	1
Hawkins, P. (R-Fla.)	4	Warner, J. (R-Va.)	1
Domenici, P. (R-N.Mex.)	3	Eagleton, T. (D-Mo.)	1
Helms, J. (R-N.C.)	3	Heinz, J. (R-Pa.)	1
Mathias, C. (R-Md.)	3	Durenberger, D. (R-Minn.)	1

Table B-11 (*continued*)

Senator	Appearances	Senator	Appearances
McClure, J. (R-Idaho)	1	Grassley, C. (R-Iowa)	0
Lautenberg, F. (D-N.J.)	1	Stafford, R. (R-Vt.)	0
Pryor, D. (D-Ark.)	1	Evans, D. (R-Wash.)	0
Andrews, M. (R-N.Dak.)	1	Huddleston, W. (D-Ky.)	0
Chafee, J. (R-R.I.)	1	Inouye, D. (D-Hawaii)	0
Danforth, J. (R-Mo.)	1	Riegle, D. (D-Mich.)	0
Rudman, W. (R-N.H.)	1	Johnston, J. (D-La.)	0
Humphrey, G. (R-N.H.)	1	Quayle, D. (R-Ind.)	0
Wallop, M. (R-Wyo.)	1	Boschwitz, R. (R-Minn.)	0
Melcher, J. (D-Mont.)	1	Mitchell, G. (D-Maine)	0
Murkowski, F. (R-Alaska)	1	Zorinsky, E. (D-Nebr.)	0
Trible, P. (R-Va.)	1	Boren, D. (D-Okla.)	0
Baucus, M. (D-Mont.)	1	DeConcini, D. (D-Ariz.)	0
Ford, W. (D-Ky.)	1	Stennis, J. (D-Miss.)	0
Mattingly, M. (R-Ga.)	1	Bingaman, J. (D-N.Mex.)	0
Sasser, J. (D-Tenn.)	1	Randolph, J. (D-W.Va.)	0
Dixon, A. (D-Ill.)	1	Burdick, Q. (D-N.Dak.)	0
Heflin, H. (D-Ala.)	1	Abdnor, J. (R-S.Dak.)	0
Pell, C. (D-R.I.)	0	Cochran, T. (R-Miss.)	0
Jepsen, R. (R-Iowa)	0	Hecht, C. (R-Nev.)	0
		Matsunaga, S. (D-Hawaii)	0

Source: "Network Roundup," a daily compilation of television appearances prepared by the Senate Republican Conference. The compilation covers fifty programs (primarily interview programs). The period surveyed included 268 days from July 1983 through June 1984.

Table B-12. *National Media Ranking*, 1983[a]

Senator	Newspapers	TV news	Sunday TV	Combined score
Glenn, J. (D-Ohio)	439	118	6	563
Cranston, A. (D-Calif.)	254	91	9	354
Baker, H. (R-Tenn.)	153	148	15	316
Dole, R. (R-Kans.)	208	87	12	307
Hart, G. (D-Colo.)	163	63	3	229
Hollings, E. (D-S.C.)	118	50	3	171
Kennedy, E. (D-Mass.)	70	86	3	159
Helms, J. (R-N.C.)	90	56	0	146
Domenici, P. (R-N.Mex.)	96	36	6	138
Moynihan, D. (D-N.Y.)	59	43	12	114
Jackson, H. (D-Wash.)	60	46	6	112
Tower, J. (R-Tex.)	50	45	12	107
Mathias, C. (R-Md.)	42	60	3	105
Percy, C. (R-Ill.)	40	62	0	102
Dodd, C. (D-Conn.)	35	46	15	96
Laxalt, P. (R-Nev.)	37	46	6	89
Byrd, R. (D-W.Va.)	32	41	3	76
Hatch, O. (R-Utah)	58	18	0	76
Tsongas, P. (D-Mass.)	26	49	0	75
Goldwater, B. (R-Ariz.)	29	25	3	57
Kasten, R. (R-Wis.)	35	20	0	55
Nunn, S. (D-Ga.)	22	21	12	55
Packwood, B. (R-Oreg.)	32	17	3	52
Metzenbaum, H. (D-Ohio)	15	32	0	47
Hatfield, M. (R-Oreg.)	28	16	0	44
Chiles, L. (D-Fla.)	24	16	3	43
Bumpers, D. (D-Ark.)	24	18	0	42
Levin, C. (D-Mich.)	14	27	0	41
Stevens, T. (R-Alaska)	30	8	3	41
Weicker, L. (R-Conn.)	19	22	0	41
Armstrong, W. (R-Colo.)	13	19	6	38
D'Amato, A. (R-N.Y.)	23	11	0	34
Biden, J. (D-Del.)	15	14	3	32
Pell, C. (D-R.I.)	16	15	0	31
Long, R. (D-La.)	18	13	0	31

Table B-12 (*continued*)

Senator	Newspapers	TV news	Sunday TV	Combined score
McClure, J. (R-Idaho)	17	14	0	31
Garn, J. (R-Utah)	25	3	3	31
Kassebaum, N. (R-Kans.)	24	4	3	31
Heinz, J. (R-Pa.)	20	10	0	30
Leahy, P. (D-Vt.)	8	16	6	30
Thurmond, S. (R-S.C.)	17	11	0	28
Warner, J. (R-Va.)	12	16	0	28
Roth, W. (R-Del.)	20	7	0	27
Eagleton, T. (D-Mo.)	21	5	0	26
Gorton, S. (R-Wash.)	11	15	0	26
Specter, A. (R-Pa.)	17	9	0	26
Grassley, C. (R-Iowa)	13	12	0	25
Simpson, A. (R-Wyo.)	22	0	3	25
Wilson, P. (R-Calif.)	16	9	0	25
Lugar, R. (R-Ind.)	13	8	3	24
Riegle, D. (D-Mich.)	7	17	0	24
Evans, D. (R-Wash.)	19	4	0	23
Stafford, R. (R-Vt.)	13	10	0	23
Chafee, J. (R-R.I.)	7	9	3	19
Danforth, J. (R-Mo.)	7	9	3	19
Durenberger, D. (R-Minn.)	18	1	0	19
Bradley, B. (D-N.J.)	16	3	0	19
Sarbanes, P. (D-Md.)	8	11	0	19
Andrews, M. (R-N.Dak.)	10	5	3	18
Denton, J. (R-Ala.)	13	2	3	18
Proxmire, W. (D-Wis.)	5	10	3	18
Cohen, W. (R-Maine)	9	8	0	17
Bentsen, L. (D-Tex.)	11	5	0	16
Lautenberg, F. (D-N.J.)	13	3	0	16
Jepsen, R. (R-Iowa)	6	9	0	15
Quayle, D. (R-Ind.)	5	10	0	15
Hawkins, P. (R-Fla.)	11	2	0	13
Inouye, D. (D-Hawaii)	7	6	0	13
Rudman, W. (R-N.H.)	7	6	0	13
Melcher, J. (D-Mont.)	3	3	6	12

Table B-12 (continued)

Senator	Newspapers	TV news	Sunday TV	Combined score
Sasser, J. (D-Tenn.)	1	8	3	12
Boschwitz, R. (R-Minn.)	5	6	0	11
Cochran, T. (R-Miss.)	9	2	0	11
Pressler, L. (R-S.Dak.)	4	7	0	11
East, J. (R-N.C.)	6	4	0	10
Johnston, J. (D-La.)	6	4	0	10
DeConcini, D. (D-Ariz.)	3	3	3	9
Randolph, J. (D-W.Va.)	2	7	0	9
Wallop, M. (R-Wyo.)	5	4	0	9
Huddleston, W. (D-Ky.)	8	0	0	8
Stennis, J. (D-Miss.)	3	5	0	8
Mitchell, G. (D-Maine)	5	2	0	7
Pryor, D. (D-Ark.)	2	4	0	6
Zorinsky, E. (D-Nebr.)	5	1	0	6
Baucus, M. (D-Mont.)	2	3	0	5
Exon, J. (D-Nebr.)	3	2	0	5
Humphrey, G. (R-N.H.)	5	0	0	5
Boren, D. (D-Okla.)	4	0	0	4
Ford, W. (D-Ky.)	2	2	0	4
Heflin, H. (D-Ala.)	0	4	0	4
Mattingly, M. (R-Ga.)	2	2	0	4
Trible, P. (R-Va.)	2	2	0	4
Bingaman, J. (D-N.Mex.)	2	1	0	3
Murkowski, F. (R-Alaska)	3	0	0	3
Symms, S. (R-Idaho)	3	0	0	3
Nickles, D. (R-Okla.)	2	0	0	2
Burdick, Q. (D-N.Dak.)	1	0	0	1
Hecht, C. (R-Nev.)	0	1	0	1
Abdnor, J. (R-S.Dak.)	0	0	0	0
Dixon, A. (D-Ill.)	0	0	0	0
Matsunaga, S. (D-Hawaii)	0	0	0	0

Source: National Newspaper Index for Christian Science Monitor, Los Angeles Times, New York Times, Wall Street Journal, Washington Post; Television News Index of Vanderbilt University for ABC, CBS, NBC evening news; and "Face The Nation" (CBS), "This Week with David Brinkley" (ABC), "Meet The Press" (NBC).

a. See pp. 12–13 for an explanation of the system used for ranking.

Index